MW00991811

Learning to Hear God's Voice

Other books by the author:

Christian Maturity and the Spirit's Power
Voice of God
Your Dreams: God's Neglected Gift

Learning to Hear God's Voice

HERMAN RIFFEL

Published by
chosen books
FLEMING H. REVELL COMPANY
OLD TAPPAN, NEW JERSEY

Scripture quotations, unless otherwise indicated, are from the New American Standard Bible, copyright © The Lockman Foundation 1960, 1962, 1963, 1968, 1971, 1972, 1973, 1975, 1977.

Additional versions used are:
Holy Bible: New International Version (North American Edition). Copyright © 1973, 1978, 1984, by the International Bible Society. Used by permission of Zondervan Bible Publishers.
New English Bible, copyright © 1961, 1970 by the Delegates of the Oxford University Press and the Syndics of the Cambridge University Press.
The Living Bible, copyright © 1971 by Tyndale House Publishers, Wheaton, Illinois.

Library of Congress Cataloging in Publication Data

Riffel, Herman H.
  Learning to hear God's voice.

  1. Revelation. 2. Christian life—Baptist authors. 3. Riffel, Herman H. I. Title
BT127.2.R526   1986   231.7'4   85-28034
ISBN 0-8007-9053-7

Edited by Leonard E. LeSourd
Designed by Ann Cherryman

A Chosen Book
Copyright © 1986 by Fleming H. Revell Company
Chosen Books are Published by
Fleming H. Revell Company
Old Tappan, New Jersey
Printed in the United States of America

To our son, David
our daughter-in-law, Marian
and our three "grand" sons
Robert, Kirk, and Craig
who have sought to hear
what the Lord is saying to them

I acknowledge my indebtedness to my editor, Leonard LeSourd, who has directed my course in writing and has become a personal friend, and to my wife, Lillie, who has shared life and fellowship and joy with me in the experiences described in this book, and to the many people, including missionaries, pastors, professors, and others, who have listened to my lectures on this subject and given valuable contributions from their experiences.

CONTENTS

PREFACE

There is increasing interest among thousands of Christians today to learn to hear the voice of God clearly and reliably. When my wife and I travel in many countries ministering to missionaries, the question asked most frequently is, "How do you distinguish the voice of God from the many other voices that you hear?" Not only missionaries and clergy pursue this subject; lay people as well realize it is crucial to our spiritual survival to be able to hear God's instructions and obey them.

My first book on the subject, *Voice of God*, defended the premise that we can hear the voice of God today. In this follow-up book I seek to explain *how* we can hear it. The answers that I present come not out of academic studies, but out of the difficult experiences of life, and out of the observations of others who are also learning to listen.

So, *Learning to Hear God's Voice* is an update on a huge subject. I urge you to explore it.

Herman Riffel

Learning to Hear God's Voice

1

Does God Still Speak Today?

I have often heard people make statements like these: "God told me to get up early this morning." "God told me to prepare a good breakfast." "God told me to work hard today." "God told me to buy this car."

There is such a matter-of-fact tone in their voices that it makes me wonder: Do instructions like these really come from a voice from heaven? If so, where does common sense fit in?

For thirty years I have been aware of my need for God's guidance in how I live my life. As our world has become more chaotic, my efforts to know God's voice have intensified.

Nor am I alone in this, I have discovered over the past year, as I have talked to dozens of people to ascertain how they feel God speaks to them.

One of these, Daryl, a returned missionary, was having difficulty with his air conditioner. He wanted to fix it himself but could not loosen the set screws. Though he called both air conditioner contractors and repairmen, none could help him.

"Suddenly," he told me, "an idea popped into my head: *Go see Bill*. And I did. Bill told me I'd have to get a

11

new fan blade, and he promised to try to find one for me. Well, he couldn't find a new one, but he found a used one in good condition, which suited me better, and he even installed it for me."

Was the idea that popped into Daryl's mind God's idea? It certainly was a good one.

Noline, a businesswoman, told me this story: "My husband and I employed a young man in order to try to help him face responsibility, but he responded by burning down our house. Then we learned that his father had a warrant out for his arrest for forgery. My husband had one of those 'holy hunches' that the young man was about to do further damage in a particular place in town, and spoke to the city detective. The detective went where my husband had suggested, and there he was. We still pray for this young man but realize he needs to be institutionalized to keep him from doing more damage."

Lee, who had gotten her job to help with her daughter's college expenses, was at work in the hangar of an Air Force base. "One day when I was about to climb two flights of concrete steps," she explained, "I had a sudden feeling that I should ask someone to go with me, since I was not feeling quite right. I responded to that impression and asked a woman to accompany me. On the way up I fainted, and she kept me from falling. I was taken to the hospital in an ambulance. Had I not listened to that inner voice, I could have fallen down nearly two stories to the concrete floor below."

Who was directing these voices, impressions, and ideas? Could it have been God?

To many today, the idea of hearing God's voice is presumptuous and self-deceiving. Our rationalistic society, permeated by Aristotelian philosophy and Freudian psychology, brands as ill or off-base anyone who claims to hear any but human voices.

To be sure, a psychologically unbalanced person may hear inner voices that tell him lies about himself and cause him to do destructive things. But most of us would have to admit that even as healthy, presumably balanced people, we hear many "voices" out of our own inner conflicts. For instance, we may hear the strong voice of our own desire to acquire a particular item. The voice of reason may counter that we cannot afford that luxury. Then the voice of selfishness may urge us to be good to ourselves, and the voice of temptation may call us to fulfill our wishes. But the voice of conscience may object, or the voice of an old authority may call us back to harsh legalism.

If we're honest, we will admit we hear plenty of voices—not audible ones, but voices nonetheless. Is it wrong to assume we can hear God's voice as well?

Jesus answers this for us in John 10:27: "My sheep hear My voice, and I know them and they follow Me."

But suppose Jesus directed this statement specifically, exclusively, to His disciples? What if, after Jesus proved Himself to be God manifest in the flesh and left this earth, and demonstrated His power to the early Church in the book of Acts, the miracles ceased? In such a case, wouldn't the miracle of hearing Him speak personally also have ceased?

After all, you and I both have heard people make comments like the following: "I want to follow the Lord and do His will, but it is enough to read the Scriptures and hear God speak through them. He isn't offering any new 'revelations' today."

As a matter of fact, that is the very concept I was taught at home, in my church, and later in school as I prepared for the ministry. I learned about the many wonderful works that Jesus did, and greatly appreciated the teaching of the Scriptures that I received. I was also told that that period of verbal communication was now over, that Jesus spoke personally while He walked on earth, but now only through the medium of the Bible.

In spite of this teaching by leaders I respected, it troubled me that the idea of no more personal communication seemed to contradict what Jesus further said to His followers: "I will ask the Father, and He will give you another Helper, that He may be with you *forever*. . . . The Helper, the Holy Spirit, whom the Father will send in My name, He will teach you all things" (John 14:16, 26, italics added).

How would the Holy Spirit teach us, if not through communication? Or how, indeed, would we as followers of Jesus "hear His voice"?

As I struggled with the question of God speaking today, I searched for more scriptural guidelines and found this declaration: "Love never fails; but if there are gifts of prophecy, they will be done away; if there are tongues, they will cease; if there is knowledge, it will be done away. For we know in part, and we prophesy in part" (1 Corinthians 13:8–9).

Just when will these gifts of the Lord be "done away"? The answer comes in the next verse: "When the perfect comes, the partial will be done away."

I knew that in heaven things will be perfect. We will not need works of healing, for instance, for heaven allows no sickness. But it is evident that perfection has not yet come on this earth, and until it does Jesus has promised that the Helper, the Holy Spirit, will continue to speak to us.

Still, convinced that this was true, my twentieth-century rational mind raised another question: Were we not to use sensory knowledge as well as reason, and to be aware of both feelings and intuition in the process of guidance? And I began at last to sort through all the ways God uses to speak to us.

God has indeed created us with five senses, like five antennae, to receive information. That we gain knowledge from that realm is undeniable because we have physical bodies and live in a material world. We can see things with our eyes, hear them with our ears, feel them, smell them, and taste them. We live in the world around us primarily by the messages that come from these senses.

God has also given us minds to use for reasoning power. The information gathered from material science, philosophy, and psychology comes mostly through the mind. God expects us to develop our minds and use them, although danger comes when our minds are not submitted to God's Spirit. The apostle Paul warned the Colossians: "See to it that no one takes you captive through philosophy and empty deception." So we need to learn to discern *who is speaking* through our minds.

Emotions and feelings are also important. Jesus had compassion on the multitudes who were hungry and were as sheep without a shepherd. This feeling of compassion compelled Him to give them food.

One housewife I know feels that God speaks to her through her emotions. "When the Lord is after me to pray for someone," she says, "I feel a deep, deep compassion for that person—much stronger than I would normally have. I cannot get away from it; I have to pray."

Other people possess that faculty of insight called intuition. God often uses this channel as He corrects our natural intuition and give us spiritual perception. We need to be on guard here, however, because Satan may find a way into this channel, too.

Satan, we need to remember, is the Deceiver. His voice can confuse believers just as readily as it did one young man I know. He heard a voice one day that said, "If you trust me, you can close your eyes when you drive."

He was confused by the directive, but was counseled, fortunately, that God will never test anyone's trust by endangering other lives. In a later chapter we will cover the ways we can check out whether it is God's voice we are hearing or the Deceiver's.

Once we have accepted the idea that it is possible to hear God's voice today, we should not be surprised to run across resistance to or prejudice against that idea. Thus it has been throughout the centuries. Even the older brother and sister of Moses had doubts about his hearing the voice of God, and said, "Has the Lord indeed spoken only through Moses? Has He not spoken through us as well?"

It would have been hard for Moses to defend himself against such a complaint, but God Himself took up the argument. He called the three of them before Him and said, "With My servant Moses, [who] is faithful in all My household; with him I speak mouth to mouth, even openly, and not in dark sayings, and he beholds the form of the Lord. Why then were you not afraid to speak against My servant, against Moses?" (Numbers 12:7–8).

I do not believe, then, that the person who listens to

the voice of God needs to worry about defending himself. He needs but to learn to hear God accurately, *and express it judiciously;* and then God will defend him.

Understand that when we are born again into the family of God, the Spirit of God awakens our human spirit: "The one who joins himself to the Lord is one spirit with Him" (1 Corinthians 6:17). It is in this realm that we recognize the voice of God. The person who has not come into spiritual life by receiving Jesus Christ as his Lord and Savior is still in the natural realm. "But a natural man does not accept the things of the Spirit of God; for they are foolishness to him, and he cannot understand them, because they are spiritually appraised" (1 Corinthians 2:14).

There is no question in my mind that if we so desire we can hear the voice of God today. I am convinced that God has always spoken to us—and in innumerable ways. I find no Scripture that indicates He spoke only in Bible times, or during the life of Jesus, or in the early Church, or before the Bible was written.

It is quite possible, therefore, that God does direct men and women to get up early on a particular morning, or to prepare a good breakfast that day for a very special reason. God might choose to communicate through a rational thought, or a loving feeling, or an intuitive process.

If the Lord speaks to us in many ways, then, not only should we be grateful that He does, but we should make it a top priority to hear His voice every day of our lives—and then to act upon His direction.

2

Why Would God Want To Speak to Me?

Our God is loving, warm-hearted, gregarious, fond of the company of others. He loves life and wants to share all of it with us.

If you are a husband and father, God is there to greet you first thing in the morning to give peace to your mind and heart and make it a good day. He wants to talk to you while you are shaving. He delights to sing with you in the shower. He is interested in the clothes you select for the day, for He even knows who you will meet at work that day. He is with you when you are tempted to be disturbed by the lateness of the hour and the pressing questions of your wife and children while you are preoccupied with an important problem you have to face at your job that day.

If you are a housewife preparing breakfast for your family, Jesus stands by to keep you at peace, even though your husband is in a hurry and the toast is burning. He wants to talk to the children through you as they interrupt your preparation to ask which socks to wear. He sees and enjoys your beauty while you are fixing your hair. He delights in you and wants to add beauty to your inner person to make you as real as you want to be.

If you are a teenager, God cares about what you do;

He wants to help you resist the temptation of the day. He sees your inner struggle as you wonder whether you dare to explain your problem to your mother or dad. It may be that they will not understand, but He does. Go ahead, talk to Him. He will not only understand, but He will give you a solution that will surprise you.

How do I know God is that kind of God? Because Jesus was that kind of person, and in Jesus God shows us what He is like. Think of that familiar day when Jesus was visiting the home of Mary and Martha. Martha was hurrying about preparing the meal, "distracted with all her preparations," while Mary "was listening to the Lord's word, seated at His feet."

When Martha could stand it no longer she said to Jesus, "Lord, do You not care that my sister has left me to do all the serving alone? Then tell her to help me."

But the Lord responded, "Martha, Martha, you are worried and bothered about so many things; but only a few things are necessary, really only one, for Mary has chosen the good part, which shall not be taken away from her" (Luke 10:41–42). Listening to Jesus' voice was "the good part" Mary had chosen.

So often we worry and talk among ourselves about many things, when there is just one thing necessary—that we be quiet and listen to what God has to say about our needs and problems. He knows the responsibility parents face to provide food and clothes and pay the mortgage on the house. Jesus said, "Your heavenly Father knows that you need all these things."

I feel sad about those individuals who believe God is all-powerful, yet silent. There are enough people worship-

ing stony gods who have mouths but cannot speak. The
psalmist says of these idols:

> They have mouths, but they cannot speak; they
> have eyes, but they cannot see; they have ears,
> but they cannot hear; they have noses, but they
> cannot smell; they have hands, but they cannot
> feel; they have feet, but they cannot walk; they
> cannot make a sound with their throat.
>
> (Psalm 115:5–7)

In fact, our God speaks to His people in many personal
ways. "He who loves Me shall be loved by My Father,"
said Jesus, "and I will love him, and will disclose Myself to
him" (John 14:21). And Jesus promised that the Helper,
the Holy Spirit, would teach us all things (John 14:26).

God wants to speak to us because He is vitally interested
in us. He has in mind things for us we cannot even
imagine. He even plans for us to be like Him, as unlikely as
that now seems. After all, we were made in His image. And
He promises that if we will cooperate with Him, He will
restore that image to perfection.

Jesus said, "You are to be perfect as your heavenly
Father is perfect." We sigh; that seems impossible now.

But this perfection is similar to when a mother says to
her little two-year-old child, "You are a perfect darling."
He may well have perfect behavior for a two-year-old
child, although if he still acts like a two-year-old when he is
eight, he is not growing as he should. That is the kind of
perfection Jesus was talking about. He does not expect us
to be perfect all at once, but He does want us to grow into
proper maturity. He says He will be with us in the process,
that He will never forsake us.

In another way, too, it is like young children and their mothers. At the heart of all the care, concern, training, and enjoyment is communication. It is vital for the little one to know the mother's voice. So it is with us and God: we must know His voice. He wants to communicate with us. He longs for intimate fellowship with us.

There is not a problem or a burden He is not aware of. There is not a pain or loss that He does not want to talk about with us, so that He can comfort and heal us. He wants to enter into our joys, feast at our table, and be a gracious guest at our meals, so that He can share His love with us.

This is how one of our friends expressed it: "The voice of God to me is an affirmative, simple, declarative sentence that I know is truth. It is always positive, reassuring, reaffirming—probably because I am a questioning person, seeing the negative side of every problem. The Lord comes to me with encouragement."

Some time back my wife, Lillie, and I were involved in a traveling ministry that took us out of the country for months at a time. In the midst of our travels we had no permanent home. For twenty-two months we lived out of suitcases while our furniture was in storage. We grew weary from the inconvenience and badly needed a home where we could settle in between our trips. But although we had looked and looked at houses in the suburbs of Detroit, we had not found what we needed, and had only a limited number of weeks in which to search.

One day as I was going to look at yet another house, feeling that nothing would be accomplished by it, a clear thought came to my mind, almost as if it had been spoken aloud: *Do you know what you want?*

No, I had to admit, I didn't know what I wanted. I knew only what I didn't want. And when I returned to our temporary quarters I told Lillie about the experience.

"What do you think we should do about it?" she asked.

"I think we need to decide what it is we really want."

She looked quizzical. "Do you think God is going to give us everything we want?"

"I don't know, but I do know that He knows our needs, and has promised to give us even our material needs if we seek His Kingdom first."

So we sat down and considered carefully what we needed. Our prayer list eventually included a quiet place to rest and recuperate after we returned from long, exhausting trips; an efficient kitchen for Lillie; a private study for me; a living room large enough to accommodate group meetings (we would have liked a fireplace but didn't ask for it); sufficient bedrooms and bathroom facilities for our guests; and enough storage space. Because we are often away from home, we asked that this dream house have the necessary care and protection when we were gone. Somewhat hesitantly we added our desire for some privacy, like a half-acre of woods nearby where we could walk and meditate.

I was a bit surprised at how specific we could be when we had to be!

We still had a few weeks to search, when "our" house became available unexpectedly at a price we could afford. It had an efficient kitchen, a comfortable study, a thirty-two-foot-long living room/dining room with a fireplace. There were extra bedrooms, a bath for guests, and plenty of storage space. Since the house was on a small conference grounds, it was watched by a caretaker. Yet it was very private, surrounded by ten thousand acres of state forest and open lands, instead of the half-acre we had haltingly asked for!

Why should God want to talk to us and hear our requests? Because He is a loving "daddy" interested in His children's every need. Though He is a Father in heaven, He has come very close to us through Jesus. Since Jesus was tempted in all things when on earth, He knows all the emotions we are going through.

Why does God want to talk with us about all our problems? Because He loves us.

3

Why Should I Try to Listen?

"Our future will begin with a call from space."

This was the closing sentence of a recent documentary about research on interplanetary communication. Though many do not recognize it, that voice from outer space has already spoken. It is the voice of God. There are many reasons why we need to learn to listen to it.

One reason is that we will get help in doing our jobs in the work-a-day world. I learned this as a hospital chaplain. For my work I found it necessary to ascertain the patients' spiritual condition so that I could try to help them. In order to do that I needed to ask the right questions.

If I asked whether they were members of a church, their answer might indicate they had made a spiritual decision. On the other hand, it might only indicate a gesture made to the church community or to their parents, not necessarily to God. If I asked whether they had been baptized, their answer might suggest an act of faith on the part of their parents or themselves, but it might not indicate whether they had responded to it with their hearts. If I asked whether they were "saved" or "born again," the question itself would have a different meaning to some than to others.

In praying about this, the Lord provided me with exactly the right questions. I was to ask the patients whether their communication with God was one-way or two-way. If it was one-way, they only talked to God. If it was two-way, they talked with God and God also talked with them. When I found some who experienced two-way communication with God, I knew there was real life within them.

In the hospital I talked to a woman in obvious pain who had suffered a great deal going through surgery. I noticed, however, that there was a sense of peace about her.

"Many of your friends from the church have been praying for you," I said to her. "Has the Lord said anything to you during this time?"

"Oh, yes," she replied. "The Lord spoke to me from a Scripture portion that came to memory. I had not thought of it for a long time, but it just seemed to spring into mind."

"What was it?"

"He reminded me that He had said, 'I will never leave you nor forsake you.' That word was so real to me, it was just as if someone in the room was speaking to me. Yes, even more real than that. It gave me comfort and assurance that He would take me through this trial."

Then I knew that this woman had a two-way communication with God. Learning to listen had given her not only a foundation enabling her to withstand pain and fear, but also the ability to witness to others triumphantly about her experiences.

Thus we have a second reason for trying to listen for God's voice. Not only will we receive help from God in our work—as I often sensed His guidance in my work as chaplain—but He will give us unspeakable comfort.

If each of us would be totally honest, I think we would admit that our hearts cry out for intimate love and fellowship. Our mates, families, or close friends may supply this to some extent, but ultimately it is God we seek for total satisfaction. In this process we need to try to hear Him. We may possess all the luxuries of a comfortable home, or the money to buy the pleasures of life and travel to the ends of the earth to see all things, yet none of these can satisfy the deepest desire of our hearts. For that we turn to God.

But God can seem so far away. We cannot see Him with our eyes, we cannot touch Him with our hands. He often seems formless and vague. If we are to have that ultimate experience of love with Him, two-way communication must be realized.

I see an analogy here between the lonely heart seeking God and the tiny life surrounded by darkness in the mother's womb. To that baby it would seem impossible that he or she would soon be free from the darkness and able to move about—not to mention learn to walk and then speak and finally become a man or woman. Yet that child is made in the image of the father and mother, and he or she has all the equipment already to develop physically, emotionally, and spiritually.

In the same way we are made in the image of God; we have already within us the potential to be like Him. As the mother speaks to her child before he or she is even born, so God speaks to us from our very inception. Perhaps He even speaks us into being. We need only to listen and imitate the whispers of God to our souls. He will be delighted even as a mother is delighted with the first sounds her child makes.

A mother is thrilled to hear the first cry of her child, but she does not remain satisfied with that. She wants communication. She wants to know that her child is hearing her as she expresses her love and care, so that he is soothed and comforted. Similarly, God does not want us to be needlessly anxious or fearful, but wants to know that we are hearing Him and learning of His care.

Linda, a writer I know, told me this: "Hearing God's voice was the one area in which Satan tormented me, because I wasn't sure I was hearing the voice of Jesus. Yet He had said, 'My sheep hear My voice.' Then one day the Lord spoke to my heart in His still, small voice. He said, 'You don't have to be too concerned about hearing My voice. It isn't that My sheep are such good listeners; it's that I'm such a good caller. When I want you to hear something, you will.' As I looked back, I knew this was true. While I did not always obey Him, when He wanted me to know something, He had made it very clear to my spirit."

At first a child in the home only imitates the sounds he hears others making. Then, as he begins to pick up the meanings, he begins to use words like *Mama* and *bottle,* as simple as they sound, to express his desires.

So God is eagerly waiting for us to listen to Him and ask for His help, even in feeble phrases that do not sound much like prayer. God loves and understands us better than any mother understands the seemingly unintelligible sounds of her little one.

But learning two-way communication with God does not

come without practice any more than does the communication between a mother and child. With practice we gradually learn to hear Him and understand His promises. When this begins to happen, we are ready to move into a deeper relationship with Him, which brings the joy of personal communication.

If I do not learn to hear and recognize God's voice and understand what He says, I am like a paralyzed child who remains helpless in spite of all his mother tries to do for him. Learning to respond to the voice that comes to us is a risk, but it is risking the natural and temporal for the spiritual and eternal.

Louisa has a special gift for ministering to people for inner healing. I asked her not long ago, "How do *you* hear the voice of God?"

She pondered the question for a long minute. "When I realized that I had a degree of hope but not much faith, I decided to take five minutes of silence per day to move from hope to faith. That was a big step for me at that time."

"What did you do in that five minutes?"

"I would take pencil and paper to jot down what I felt the Lord might be saying to me. I would also jot down my thoughts about other things to do, to be able to put those things aside. Then I would separate the two lists."

"How long did it take you until you could hear and recognize God's voice?"

"After nine months," she responded carefully, "I heard the Lord say, 'Now you know My voice.' "

"Did you ever wonder after that whether the voice you heard was really God's voice?"

"Oh, many times! I didn't always know whether it was my voice or God's. But the more I kept at it, the easier it became."

Keeping at it is critically important. Towering personalities in the Bible learned that their futures could depend on what they heard God say to them. On specific instruction, Abraham left his home, family, and possessions to go to another land occupied by other peoples, expecting God to fulfill His word. When it had never yet rained, Noah built a huge ship on dry land from the plans he believed God gave him. Joseph heard God in a dream and fled with his wife and infant child to the strange and far-off land of Egypt. An imprisoned Paul wrote letters to the churches, giving the principles God taught him while all alone. John, a captive exile on a barren island, wrote down visions of the future that still excite and stagger the imagination.

Each of these individuals acted on what he thought God had said. Did their risks pay off? There would be no nation called Israel were it not for Abraham's risk of obedience. Noah saved the world by doing what seemed foolish to others. Joseph protected the Child who became our Savior by listening to the voice of God in a dream. Paul's letters became the chief means of instruction for churches down through twenty centuries. And John's risk of love for His Lord gave us hope for the future in this uncertain world.

Unfortunately, we do not usually become serious about listening to what God has to say to us until our situation becomes desperate. Years ago Lillie and I underwent a time of severe testing when we discovered that our daughter was missing. Eventually we had to find the answer from the Lord, for the world had no answer to our problem. Nothing else mattered, nothing else interested us. Food was forgotten and sleep would not come. How could we go on with the routine of life? We had to have an answer that would give us both direction and hope.

In our desperation we not only prayed but listened. God spoke to me then from Psalm 124, a portion of Scripture I had read many times before: "Our soul has escaped as a bird out of the snare of the trapper; the snare is broken and we have escaped. Our help is in the name of the Lord, who made heaven and earth" (verses 7–8).

This time, however, God spoke with an impression left deep within my heart: *This is a word for you regarding your daughter.*

It became a personal promise that stood with me for twenty years. Lillie also found encouragement as God spoke to her in that traumatic time. We knew that His promises would be fulfilled, for the word spoken was clear and specific to our hearts.

We need to learn to listen to God, not only so that He can speak to us in great emergencies, but so that He can guide us day by day. We need not wander for forty years as the Israelites did in the wilderness, before being ready for God to show us the way. He is willing to teach us as little children to hear His voice and learn to follow Him. Then we can leave straight tracks in the sands of time for our children to follow.

4

How Does God Speak?
Biblical Examples

Ours is a God of infinite variety and expression. He is not limited to a single language or form of communication. It is by His voice that God communicates most commonly with man. The root of the word *voice* actually means to call out with a sound. That is the word used many times by both God and man in the Scriptures.

Apparently the eternal, invisible God was real to Adam and Eve, as though they could see and touch Him, since shortly after their creation He and they were in conversation. They must have had good times as God showed them all the animals and birds and fish of the sea, and told them they were to care for and rule over them.

After the tragic turn of events, when Adam and Eve disobeyed the command of God and were ordered out of the Garden, we might have thought God would now no longer speak to them, or at least that they would be unable to hear Him. But that was not so. Even after the man and woman sinned and were ashamed, they still heard the voice of God as He walked in the garden. Though they were afraid and hid themselves, they still carried on a conversation with Him.

The Lord God called to Adam, "Why are you hiding?"

And Adam replied, "I heard you coming and didn't want you to see me naked. So I hid."

"Who told you you were naked?" the Lord God asked. "Have you eaten fruit from the tree I warned you about?"

"Yes," Adam admitted, "but it was the woman you gave me who brought me some, and I ate it."

Then the Lord God asked the woman, "How could you do such a thing?"

"The serpent tricked me," she replied.

So the Lord God said to the serpent. . . .

(Genesis 3:9–14, LB)

Conversations between God and man were the natural part of life from the beginning, sometimes recognized right away, sometimes not. (Notice that God even spoke to an animal!)

To Samuel, the little boy in the Temple, God's voice sounded like the voice of his priest. Samuel was lying down one night when the Lord called his name. In those days a word from the Lord was rare; certainly Samuel did not recognize it. He ran to Eli and said, "Here I am, for you called me."

But Eli said, "I did not call, lie down again." So Samuel went back to his bed.

The Lord called again, "Samuel."

Samuel got up and again went to Eli. "Here I am," he said, "for you called me."

Even Eli the priest did not recognize that this might be God calling, so he repeated, "I did not call, my son, lie down again."

When the Lord called him the third time, because he had not yet learned to know God's voice, he went back to Eli obediently and said, "Here I am, for you called me."

It was only then that Eli, perhaps remembering that the voice of God may sometimes sound like the voice of a man, discerned that this was the voice of God.

Other Scripture accounts indicate that God's voice sounded different at different times. Sometimes it was like a whisper, sometimes a thunderous roar, sometimes just a strong impression.

When Israel was gathered at Mt. Sinai, God spoke in a thunderous voice and with an earthquake: "Now Mount Sinai was all in smoke because the Lord descended upon it in fire; and its smoke ascended like the smoke of a furnace, and the whole mountain quaked violently. When the sound of the trumpet grew louder and louder, Moses spoke and God answered him with thunder" (Exodus 19:18–19). So terrible was the sight that Moses said, "I am full of fear and trembling" (Hebrews 12:21).

Amos had a similar perspective. A shepherd in the hills of Judea, Amos was also a prophet sent to the court of the king to give a message from God. When the king would not listen to his message, but told him to go back to his herds, Amos responded, "A lion has roared! Who will not fear? The Lord God has spoken! Who can but prophesy?" (Amos 3:8). Whether or not the king would listen, Amos considered the voice of the Lord as powerful as the roar of a lion in the wilderness.

David spoke of God's voice as if it were a great howling storm: "The voice of the Lord is powerful. The voice of the Lord is majestic. The voice of the Lord breaks the cedars. . . . The voice of the Lord hews out flames of fire. The voice of the Lord shakes the wilderness" (Psalm 29:4–5, 7–8).

The apostle John said that the voice of the risen Jesus was like the sound of many waters, perhaps like the breakers of the sea (Revelation 1:15).

God speaks in many different ways, not by voice only, and often in ways we will be sure to hear Him, if we have not closed our ears completely. But we must be willing to listen and learn to recognize His voice from all the other voices calling for our attention.

The ways God speaks to us today can perhaps be culled from five of the different ways that He spoke to Abraham: By word, by vision or dream, by another man, by an angel, and by the Holy Spirit.

We learn that God first spoke to Abraham by word when He asked him to leave his home and country for a land where He promised to make a nation of him. The word must have impressed Abraham, but it took some time for him to become fully persuaded to follow it. Finally he took his wife and servants and cattle to the country God had told him about. There he lived a nomad's life among other surrounding tribes. The voice of God by personal word to Abraham had become his first challenge.

Next, God spoke to Abraham by word through another man. When he was returning from battle to rescue Lot, his nephew, God spoke to him through Melchizedek, an unknown priest, who gave him a blessing from the most high God. Abraham was so impressed with the blessing that he later responded to a king who wanted to reward him for rescuing him like this: "I have sworn to the Lord God Most High, possessor of heaven and earth, that I will not take a thread or a sandal thong or anything that is yours, lest you should say, 'I have made Abram rich'" (Genesis 14:22–23). So Abraham recognized the voice of God as it came through a man.

Later, while Abraham with his little family and servants lived in that strange country among large nomad tribes, he became afraid. He needed encouragement, just as we all do. Then God gave him a vision, apparently in the form of a shield, saying to him, "Do not fear, Abram, I am a shield to you; your reward shall be very great" (Genesis 15:1). So this time God encouraged Abraham by showing His word by means of a vision.

All this time, Abraham had waited patiently for a child. It seemed that the time would never come when God's promise should be fulfilled. He did not have even one child, let alone the nation of which God had spoken to him. Then God put Abraham into a deep sleep. Terror and darkness fell upon him. God gave him a dream that told the future of the nation for the next four hundred years. With the dream he also made the great covenant with Abraham that still stands. So the dream became another of the ways that God's voice came to Abraham.

If we did not know ourselves so well, we might think that speaking to Abraham with an inner voice, then sending a priest with a word for him, then communicating with him by vision, and then by dream, should be enough to persuade him to depend completely on the Lord. But all

this happened over a period of many years, and Abraham
became discouraged. Sarah was still barren, so Abraham
took a slave girl to be a second wife, thinking he would help
God out. But, as in our experience when we try to help
God out, it only caused a greater problem. In fact, it
became such a great problem that it finally caused
Abraham to give up his own efforts and trust God to fulfill
his promise.

Finally, when God saw that Abraham and Sarah were
ready to trust only in Him, He sent some very special
messengers. Three men suddenly stood in front of Abraham's tent. He invited them in and asked Sarah to prepare
a meal. But before long he realized that one of them was
the Lord God, and the other two were His angels. God
communicated His great message to Abraham and Sarah
about the birth of their son through the angels.

On another occasion God took Abraham outside and
told him to "look toward heaven and count the stars," if he
could, adding, "So shall your descendants be." We do not
know exactly how God's voice came to Abraham, but it
was evidently one of those direct and unmistakable ways
the Holy Spirit speaks to man.

Overall, then, God spoke to Abraham by voice, by vision
and dream, by a man, by an angel, and by the Holy Spirit.
But it was not to Abraham alone that God spoke in these
many ways. He also spoke to Samuel, David, Elijah,
Elisha, Isaiah, Jeremiah, Ezekiel, Daniel, and the other
prophets; and to Peter, John, Paul, and many others as
well. God is not limited to a single form of communication,
which is why the New Testament writer said that God
"spoke long ago to the fathers in the prophets in many

portions and in many ways" (Hebrews 1:1). Remember that Jeremiah *felt* the voice instead of hearing it, and said it was like a fire burning in his bones.

In subsequent chapters we will take a look at current examples of many divine forms of communication, and ways to sharpen our ability to hear them.

5

Taking Time to Be
Alone with God

If only God would speak in a voice we could all recognize, it would make hearing Him so much easier!

But is that really necessary? Jesus said, "My sheep hear [recognize] My voice, and I know them, and they follow Me" (John 10:27). Concerning His sheep He says, "A stranger they simply will not follow, but will flee from him, because they do not know [recognize] the voice of strangers" (verse 5)

The most basic requirement for hearing God's voice is finding the time to be alone with Him. The heart longs deeply for time to contemplate and meditate, which is the reason so many young people have sought out Eastern religions.

There is a great difference, however, between the meditation of Eastern religions and that of Christianity. Eastern religions call for the mind to become completely empty until it reaches a Nirvana stage of freedom from the external world. In Christianity, God calls upon us to become quiet until all the outer voices are stilled, so that we can hear Him.

We can learn from the East, however, the importance of becoming quiet. The Western mind is so geared toward activity that we are persuaded we cannot afford the time it takes. We must always be *doing* something.

When God first spoke to me about taking an hour with Him each day, I found I had to resolve some persistent arguments that are common to our thinking. First of all I had to ask myself, "Is it worthwhile to spend a hour with God each day?"

"Of course it is," was my immediate response. But I knew that was only theory, for I had said it many times before. I had agreed in my mind to do it, but not with my heart. Thus, it would last only a few days until something more urgent would confront me. Then my mind would change and I would find myself back in my old routine. For a while I would feel guilty, but eventually my mind would persuade my heart not to accept guilt. Meanwhile, the battle was lost.

Now I had to begin again, for my heart was not satisfied with the shallowness of my spiritual experience. Again I asked myself the question, "Is it worthwhile to spend an hour each day with God?"

This time I considered my answer much more carefully. If I were a mathematician, I asked myself, would I consider it worthwhile to spend an hour each day with Einstein, if I could? I knew I would gladly make that a priority. In fact, I would count it a great privilege.

If I were a composer, I continued to ask myself, would I be willing to take lessons from Beethoven, if he could give me only an hour at five every morning? Again, I knew there would not be an hour of the day I would not desire to sit at the feet of that master.

Then I asked myself, "How important is God to me? Is

He less important to me than the masters of this world?"
That put the question in another light, and I began to
consider what a privilege it was to spend an hour with the
Creator of the heavens and the earth—especially since He
was not only willing but anxious to spend it with me!

Dag Hammarskjold once wrote: "How can you keep
your powers of hearing when you never want to listen?
That God should have time for you, you seem to take as
much for granted as that you cannot have time for Him.*

That helped me get started, but the battle had just
begun. My mind still had other questions to raise: When
should I take that time with God? Should I take the first
hour in the morning or the last hour of the day?

Since I am a morning person, ordinarily my best time
would be the first hour of the day. But Lillie and I were
just beginning one of our long trips of many months that
would involve innumerable changes in daily schedules, and
often living in other people's homes.

Did God really know my schedule? Was He aware of all
I had to do? What if I was too tired? I had to get sufficient
rest to stay in good health. Would I disrupt my host's
schedule? And on and on my mind argued.

I considered these questions most carefully. Then I said
to myself, "I must take the hour that the Lord calls me,
and allow no room for discussion or argument. If it is the
Lord God of heaven that calls, it is not for me to argue with
Him."

That decision required great conviction that the Lord

*Markings, Dag Hammarskjold. Epiphany, p. 7.

knew my planned schedule, that he knew what interruptions would occur each day well before I did. It also required a sternness in my decision to be unwavering. But when those questions were answered to my full satisfaction, I was able to take an hour to be alone with God.

The battle, however, was still not over. When I insisted on making it a full hour, not fifty minutes or even fifty-five, the question came: Am I not being legalistic? One thing Jesus came to set us free from, after all, was legalism.

As I considered this question, I thought of the man working his eight-hour shift in a factory. Was it legalistic for him to go to work promptly at eight each morning and stay until five in the afternoon?

The answer, of course, was no. To keep his job, he had to give the full time required.

When *would* it be legalistic? I wondered.

Perhaps if the worker came on Saturday, or Sunday, or on his day off, when not needed or expected, only because he had a compulsion to do the same thing every day over and over. But to fulfill my own assignment daily with the Lord, putting in the hours required of me, was faithfulness, not legalism.

That provided the answer for me. In fact, as I considered the necessity of taking that time apart with God, a Bible verse came to mind: "Could you . . . not keep watch with me for one hour?" (Matthew 26:40, NIV). This does not bind everyone to set aside an hour each day to be alone with God, but it was clear that He had called me to do so, for He knew what was before me.

I made my decision to spend an hour a day with the Lord in 1982, just before we departed on a year's ministry that took us to Hawaii, New Zealand, Australia, Singapore, Taiwan, and Japan. It proved to be a year filled with many changes as we moved forty-five times from one place to the next, to perform the ministry the Lord had given us. We spent only eleven days at home in the whole year.

Sometimes the Lord would awaken me and call for that hour in the middle of the night. Sometimes in the middle of an afternoon I would hear His quiet voice, "This is your hour," and I would find that His timing was perfect. What a source of peace and power that hour proved to be!

I kept it a secret, however, and did not even tell Lillie about my decision until a whole year had passed, for I did not want it to become rule or law. Rather, it became more important to me than breakfast in the morning. I had taken time most of my life to be with the Lord each day, but now it became a matter of even greater importance, though I took care not to impose it on others.

I will, however, say this: that we cannot expect to discern God's voice from all the other voices continually bombarding us unless we take time to be quiet and let all the other voices fall silent. Jesus said, "When you pray, go into your inner room, and when you have shut your door, pray to your Father who is in secret" (Matthew 6:6). My wise professor, Dr. B. B. Sutcliffe, said, "If you have an hour to spend with God and it takes you fifty minutes to 'shut the door,' it is better to spend ten minutes alone with God than sixty minutes with the door open."

When we do take time apart with God, God takes it for granted that we will recognize His voice. Just as Adam and Eve needed no lessons in order to recognize Him—He spoke to them, they heard and understood Him, and they talked with Him—it seems plain from the scriptural record that we, too, should know His voice. It is evident, however, that man lost that recognition and had to relearn it. During the time of the judges of Israel, "the word from the Lord was rare in those days, visions were infrequent" (1 Samuel 3:1).

God had to start over with the boy, Samuel, as we have already seen, to make His people aware that God still spoke to men. Eli's counsel to Samuel to reply to the voice in the Temple, "Speak, Lord, for thy servant is listening," was good advice. In fact, that is a good maxim to follow if ever a person wants to begin a conversation with God, even though God may speak through an impression, a thought, or a still, small voice.

Frank is an engineer who works at an electronics firm. He is also a sincere Christian. He decided to take some quiet time to hear the Lord on Saturday mornings. "Prior to this," he told me, "I had a very sporadic quiet time with actual months going by without any Bible reading or silent time before the Lord."

Then in prayer he "heard" a complete message, as though it had been spoken in his mind. Believing it to be the Lord, he carefully recorded it in his journal:

> My son,
> Think not that I am asking you to do the impossible. Think not that I am leading you through a valley of thorns, for where I want you to go I will be there. The task is simple in my love and well within your grasp, and I will be there to guide you. I want you to be My person at your

work—and I will give you power to solve your problems. Trust Me to lead you and I will take you to that place of ultimate fulfillment. I am the Lord, your friend.

Despite this wonderful challenge and reassurance, Frank had certain fears, which he expressed on paper in this way:

Dear Lord,
I come before you with pen in hand ready to receive what you have for me. Yet I am concerned that I will record flickers of my better judgment, high-sounding phrases, or veiled wishes from my heart. Please help me to block out these things—or let me say, Please block out these things from me, that I may hear only what You want me to write. And I ask, is it appropriate for me to presume You will speak via my written word on a regular basis? I sit before You, seeking Your best.

All my love, Frank.

The Lord loves this kind of honesty, and He answered Frank with another "thought message":

Yes, Frank, it is appropriate to wait before Me weekly, and daily, too. There is much I have to say to you and much you need to hear. I am concerned not with externals, but with internals of your life; the rest will take care of itself. I have heard your prayer and am aware of your troubled mind. Do not give your mind to idle contemplation. Do not berate yourself for being human and

having human weaknesses; I can stand that
better than a cold heart. I love you, Frank.

God is practical and interested in all our daily problems
and needs. He does not want us to put on a "spiritual"
language or appearance. He accepts us just as we are,
where we are. We may feel it is only the "spiritual" person
who can reliably hear from God, but as we see from
Frank's dialogue, that is not true.

Even Jeremiah, that mighty prophet of God, needed
reassurance from time to time that it was really God whose
voice he heard. Jeremiah had stood before kings and said
with authority, "Thus says the Lord. . . ." What's more,
what Jeremiah said, *happened*. He, too, had to listen to God,
however, just as we do. He tells about it in his book. (See
Jeremiah 32:1–6.)

When his message of warning had been rejected by the
leaders of Israel, Jeremiah was thrown into prison. While
he was imprisoned in the court of the guard, as the
Babylonian army besieged Jerusalem, a word from the
Lord came to him: "Behold, Hanamel the son of Shallum
your uncle is coming for you, saying, 'Buy for yourself my
field which is at Anathoth, for you have the right of
redemption to buy it' " (verse 7). We do not know how this
word came to Jeremiah, exactly, but he believed it was
God speaking.

Sure enough, Hanamel came just as the Lord had said.
He asked Jeremiah to buy the field. Then follows a
statement significant to us today. Jeremiah says, *"Then I
knew that this was the word of the Lord"* (verse 8, italics
added). At first Jeremiah thought he heard the Lord saying

that his cousin would come and offer him some land and that he was to buy it, but evidently he was not sure. When his cousin came, however, and did exactly as the Lord said he would do, then he *knew* that it had been the voice of the Lord. This encourages me when I think I hear the Lord speaking but am not sure it is His voice.

Jeremiah had already said that the word of the Lord had come to him.

What made him sure?

It was the confirmation that came when his cousin did exactly what the Lord said he would do. Even the great prophet who could stand before kings and declare the word of the Lord apparently still needed God's encouragement to know for sure that he had heard correctly. Isn't that just like our experiences when we think we have heard from the Lord but are not quite sure?

Nevertheless, it is when we take time alone with God, such as Jeremiah and my engineer friend Frank took, that God talks to us most frequently. It may even be through a great loss, like the death of a loved one.

This happened when God spoke in a dream to Magdalene, a bereft wife, during Christmastime a few weeks after the death of her father.

"I was awake," she explained, "but saw a scene as if from a dream. The setting was a hillside cemetery in winter, bare trees, cold, windy, and cloudy. A mutilated coffin was partially above-ground. I remembered that the coffin had been beautiful at the wake and funeral, polished to a high gloss, beautifully shaped, and a color of reddish brown. Now it was scraped, the finish gone and the wood beginning to rot. The lid was ajar and I could see my father.

"But in contrast to the condition of the coffin, Father was not touched by death. He looked as good as when I last saw his body at the wake. I marveled and felt at peace. The rotted coffin did not disturb me.

"I feel the Lord was telling me to stop seeing my father as rotting in the grave," Magdalene reflected, "that he is whole with Christ."

Magdalene's whole approach to death and resurrection was transformed by this experience of hearing God when she was alone.

Sometimes in the midst of terrible, undeserved rejection, when anger and bitterness seem about to consume us, we may hear the creative word of God, if we are willing to listen.

It was after Moses was rejected in Egypt, having to flee to the wilderness and herd sheep for forty years, that he heard God's call to the greatest task in Israel's history. Israel rejected most of its great prophets. Jesus Himself was rejected, but out of it came the redemption of all believers.

If you are afraid to go off alone to hear what God has to say to you, if you are afraid of what you will receive, be reminded of these words of Jesus:

> What man is there among you, when his son shall ask him for a loaf, will give him a stone? Or if he shall ask for a fish, he will not give him a snake, will he? If you then, being evil, know how to give good gifts to your children, how much more shall your Father who is in heaven give what is good to those who ask Him!
>
> (Matthew 7:9–11)

The treasure to be found in the quiet times alone with the Lord can seldom be found in the rush of a too-busy day.

6

How God Speaks Through Scripture

It was early in the summer of 1970 in Zurich, Switzerland. Lillie and I had been asked by missionaries from ten countries to come and minister to them. When I asked them about the dates they would like us to come, they suggested I set up the schedule the way it suited us. But how could I arrange a schedule to speak to groups of missionaries who are often away from their homes in tribal areas for months at a time? It would be impossible to arrive at the right time in all ten countries. At least it seemed so.

Nevertheless, I had the invitations and the Lord had impressed upon us to go. So I went to the airline office in Zurich and told the ticket agent I wanted to arrange a ten-month 'round-the-world trip to Lahore, Kathmandu, Bangkok, Saigon, Hong Kong, Fujinomiya, Manila, Port Moresby, Darwin, Brisbane, Sydney, Melbourne, Christchurch, and Auckland.

While I was puzzling over the schedule, a verse of Scripture kept repeating itself to me: "I will go before thee, and make the crooked places straight" (Isaiah 45:2, KJV). That phrase kept going through my mind almost like a ringing in my ears. In two hours the agent and I had set up a 'round-the-world tour including all the cities that I had asked for.

49

That schedule never needed to be changed.

That is when I first learned by experience how wonderfully the Lord arranges things if we cooperate with Him and listen to His direction. It was amazing to see how beautifully that schedule worked out. Over and over again, we arrived at just the right time. Even when one invitation was canceled, which meant that we had two weeks with no schedule and little money on the other side of the world, the Lord's timing was still right. A medical doctor had been at a dinner party with us in a brief stop in Bangkok. When he learned of the cancellation, he brought us back on a three-thousand-mile detour to minister for two weeks to sixty missionaries he felt should hear the lectures.

The Lord had brought to mind a verse of Scripture I had known for years and made it alive in me through the Holy Spirit for that occasion.

On the same trip, we arrived at one mission base the very day the annual speaker left. Since the conference had ended, many of the missionaries would be scattering to their tribal locations many miles apart. However, that too proved to be the right timing. We learned that, by his messages, the former speaker had prepared the way for our coming. Furthermore, since we were staying for four months in that place, longer than in any other, we had the joy of entering into another's work and sharing the harvest.

All this was evidently the Lord's doing. He went before us and made the crooked places straight—much "straighter," in fact, than if we had known about the missionaries' schedules and made out the "proper" plans. Thus, a promise in the Scriptures became the voice of God to me.

God has given us the Scriptures as a record of His

dealings with men from many different cultures over a period of 1,600 years. It includes experiences of men and women both good and bad, which become a pattern for good works and a warning for evil. The Bible covers the history of man from the beginning and even shows us the final outcome of world events. In it we can find the very experiences that will enlighten us concerning the problems we are facing today. So we read the Bible's history not only to gain information, but to challenge and instruct us concerning present-day events.

We are encouraged to believe God as Abel, Enoch, Noah, Abraham, Sarah, and others did. But where others failed, we are to take a lesson from the consequences of their unbelief.

God may also speak to us through the great principles of faith we find in His dealings with men and women over the generations. Solomon gathered together a book of proverbs in which are many basic principles for everyday life.

The psalmist calls us to enter into songs of praise and worship: "I will bless the Lord at all times; His praise shall continually be in my mouth" (Psalm 34:1). In the praises of God we hear Him speak.

The New Testament is filled with direct teaching for today. In the rich instruction of the Sermon on the Mount, and in His wayside teaching, Jesus speaks to all of us. In the parables He speaks to all who hear, while the rest fail to understand.

But as we seek guidance from Scripture, we must be careful to observe certain basic rules of interpretation. We must see what the text says in light of the context. If there is a question, we may need to check the translation with the original text. Then we must look to see if it falls into a cultural setting or if it is a basic principle of Scripture for all times.

Above all, to hear God speak to us from the Scriptures, we must allow the Holy Spirit to illumine God's Word. Jesus said, "When He, the Spirit of truth, comes, He will guide you into all the truth" (John 16:13). The Holy Spirit takes one portion of the Scriptures, brings it to life for us, and applies it to the present circumstances, as He did for me when I was arranging my airline schedule.

Therefore, we need to invite the Holy Spirit's direction as we read the Scriptures. Then we may read the Bible through as history and yet receive the enlightenment of the Holy Spirit upon it. We may study its great doctrines and yet not get caught in "dead theology." We can enter into the songs of the psalmist and be lifted up in praise to God. We may read the great prophets who spoke to Israel and suddenly hear the Holy Spirit say, "This is for you today."

God said long ago through the Law, for instance, that if Israel would not listen and obey His commandments, "The heaven which is over your head shall be bronze, and the earth which is under you, iron. The Lord will make the rain of your land powder and dust; from heaven it shall come down on you until you are destroyed" (Deuteronomy 28:23–24). That warning had been part of the Law for many generations, but Israel sinned and still it rained. The word of God seemed to be ineffective.

Then one day a man by the name of Elijah became deeply disturbed about Israel's sin. The Spirit of God awakened him to the word God had spoken. Elijah prayed about it until God's warning burned with fire in his heart.

Then he went directly to Ahab, the wicked king of Israel, and said, in effect, "Because of Israel's sin it will not rain until I say so" (see 1 Kings 17:1).

Just as Elijah had warned, it did not rain for three-and-a-half years. Then God spoke to Elijah again, and when Elijah spoke the word it rained again. Without the Spirit, the word of the Law had produced no fruit. But the Spirit of God brought it to life in Elijah—although James reminds us that "Elijah was a man with a nature like ours" (James 5:17). In other words, God can do it through us, too, if we will listen to Him when He speaks and do what He tells us to do.

When we meditate on the Scriptures, we may feel as the two disciples felt on the way to Emmaus when a stranger joined them. Later, when they realized it had been Jesus walking beside them, they said, "Were not our hearts burning within us while he was speaking to us on the road, while He was explaining the Scriptures to us?" (Luke 24:32). There is a great value in meditating upon the Scriptures, for it gives the Holy Spirit an opportunity to speak words of comfort, or encouragement, or challenge to us.

An officer, retired from Army service, could hardly keep the tears back when he said, "The touch of God is when He hits me with a tender heart, a sweetness of Scripture, or keenness of prayer. At noon today at work I pulled out the Bible I used in my military days. As I read I was overwhelmed with the love of Jesus as presented there, showing God's great love for sinners. Things became deeply meaningful."

There are many ways to read the Scriptures, but to hear

God speak through them we must listen with our hearts as well as our minds. So whether we read many chapters rapidly, or study a shorter passage thoroughly, or meditate upon one significant word at a time, we must always listen for what God is saying to our hearts. Only He knows the whole truth about our circumstances. He wants to reveal what is necessary. He may even want to say something to us about the next day of which we know nothing as yet.

One day when I returned to my parent's home after being away in the ministry, I was meditating on the Psalms and came to Psalm 34:1: "I will bless the Lord at all times; His praise shall continually be in my mouth." I fixed this in my mind before I went to sleep.

I awoke in the night, smelled smoke, and quickly warned my parents. That night my parents' home burned to the ground. There was nothing left but what we could grab in the dark. All the next day, however, those words from Psalm 34 stuck in my mind. I did praise the Lord that day, and the next, and the Lord worked wonders.

In the few days that I was with my parents, the Lord supplied them with a new house. Friends had built it for themselves two years before but were not using it. We laid a new foundation, moved the house onto it, and had my parents settled before I had to go back to my work. At that time I did not yet know how important praise is in the Lord's plan. But through my meditation He gave me just the word I needed for that crisis.

The Scriptures are the primary vehicle by which God is revealed to us. We must take time, therefore, to read, study, and meditate upon them, although we worship not the vehicle but the God who is revealed in it.

It is the Holy Spirit who interprets that Word of God to us. We need to listen to the Holy Spirit as we read the Scriptural record, for He will make biblical history become a pattern for our own story. He will make the Psalms become our songs. He will cause the prophets to awaken within us a message for the present day.

In it all, we will see Jesus who lived not only two thousand years ago, but also wants to live out His life in us today.

7

How God Speaks
Through Dreams

All of us dream about an hour or more each night. If we know that God did not create anything without a purpose, it stands to reason that there is a purpose in our dreaming. But in our culture we have been so taught to ignore our dreams that we have many obstacles to remove before we can hear God speak through them. Because the fact is, the dream is a safe and reliable way God uses to speak to man.

I began to learn this twenty years ago when I first heard a lecture by Morton Kelsey, an Episcopal priest who has since written widely on the subject. I was too busy to pay attention to the subject at the time. But when I heard another lecture the next year I told the Lord I was willing to listen. That very night I had a dream that portrayed my unconscious thoughts and where they would take me in such a vivid way that I knew God was speaking to me. From that time I took an interest in dreams.

I began to listen to my dreams and get some meaning from them, even though I hardly knew where to turn. I was directed to some reading that was helpful, and finally I attended some special studies at the C. G. Jung Institute for Psychological Studies in Zurich, Switzerland. As I listened to find the truths of God amid man's understanding, I found that many of the principles of dream interpretation I learned there were inherent in the Scriptures, though ignored in my personal training.

One of the things I learned was that God speaks through dreams to all people, even as he did to Pharoah and Nebuchadnezzar. The dream, however, usually reflects not the direct but the *indirect* voice of God. Just as a mirror "speaks" to us by showing us our outward conditions, so the dream speaks by showing us our *inward* conditions.

First of all, let's see what the Bible has to say about God speaking through dreams. (We will note that *dream* and *vision* are used interchangeably in Scripture, for they come from the same deep source.) We need only take an unabridged concordance to see that the Bible is filled with dreams and visions. God spoke to Abraham, Jacob, Joseph, Solomon, Isaiah, Jeremiah, Ezekiel, and all the prophets of the Old Testament, through dreams and visions.

The dream gives us messages our minds cannot or will not receive. It may be that the mind simply cannot comprehend the things God wants to say to us. Or maybe there are barriers of prejudice that do not allow the mind to accept the truth that God wants to reveal, so He shows these things to us through dreams.

A vision shows us what cannot be seen with our physical eyes. Many people think a vision is a look at something that is not really there. On the contrary, it is a reality that is veiled or blocked from our sight until God gives us the ability to see it. The vision and the dream need proper interpretation, of course, but God uses them both to show us many hidden truths.

The New Testament opens with five dreams and three visions surrounding the Christmas story:

When the priest Zacharias and his wife, Elizabeth, considered themselves too old to have a child, God gave Zacharias a vision through an angel that Elizabeth was to bear a child who would become John the Baptist.

Because it was impossible for Mary to comprehend that she could be the mother of the Son of God, especially while she was still a virgin, God sent her confirmation of this in a vision of the angel Gabriel.

Joseph's mind could not accept the message he received about Mary becoming the mother of the Messiah, so God sent an angel to him in a dream. Later, through a dream he was directed to go to Egypt with his little family; through a dream he was told when to return and where to live.

The wise men, too, were given insights beyond human understanding through a dream.

So we see that visions and dreams are often carriers of important messages. In addition, God had said specifically to Moses, Aaron, and Miriam: "If there is a prophet among you, I, the Lord, will make Myself known to him in a vision. I shall speak with him in a dream" (Numbers 12:6). He did so with the prophets consistently, both in the Old Testament and with John in Revelation.

Lest we think we do not need to take notice of dreams today since we have the Holy Spirit, let us take note of what Peter prophesied at Pentecost, based on the prophet Joel: "I will pour forth of My Spirit upon all mankind . . . and your young men shall see visions, and your old men shall dream dreams" (Acts 2:17). Thus, dreams and visions are related to the work of the Holy Spirit in this very day.

We may well ask why we in Western culture have
ignored dreams and visions. In my opinion, it is because of
Aristotelian philosophy that said valid knowledge can
come only from the five senses and from reason. This
philosophy invaded Western culture until it infected the
Church. And it is for this reason that much of the Western
Church has so resisted the supernatural realm, including
miracles, the manifestations (or gifts) of the Holy Spirit,
and dreams and visions. Eastern culture, whatever wrong
ideas it may have advanced, has never denied these
supernatural manifestations of God.

We must again recognize that what God has done in the
supernatural realm in the past, He continues to do today
by His Spirit. As He has always spoken through dreams
and visions, so He continues to do, but we must be willing
to listen.

And to understand the dream and the vision, we need to
learn its elementary language. While the mind speaks
through concepts and reason, the dream speaks a language
of pictures and symbols. Although it is a simple language,
it is universal (like picture-roadsigns or cartoons) as well as
symbolic, and must not be interpreted rationally.

Often we hear people say when speaking of an unusual
action in a dream, "But that couldn't really happen."
What they mean is that it could not happen if interpreted
literally. Pharoah of Egypt dreamed of seven thin cows
devouring seven fat ones. Joseph did not interpret his
dream literally, as though it were a weight-watcher's
dream, but symbolically. (The seven fat cows represented
seven years of plenty and the thin ones seven years of
famine.) This symbolic interpretation not only made good
sense but proved to be true.

Space does not permit a full study of the subject of dreams, of course. This has already been done from a biblical approach.* We need to know, however, that the dream speaks naturally of the inner life. When we dream of our childhood house, the dream is most likely taking us back to the psychological house of our childhood—perhaps the environment of the soul, or the training, or the inner feelings of those days. When we dream of falling, we must ask ourselves whether we have left "solid ground" and are in a precarious position inwardly.

Adults often say that they dream only of their work at home or in the office, and young people may dream of school. There is a reason for this: the dream draws its symbols from the dreamer. Thus Joseph, who was a herdsman, dreamed of sheaves of grain and stars of the night. King Nebuchadnezzar dreamed of a statue with which he had close associations. We must find the meaning of the symbol, as well as the dream, from the dreamer.

When Lillie and I were in the interior of Zaire we heard the dreams of African pastors. One discouraged pastor said, "Just before I came to this conference I dreamed that I was in my dugout canoe and it was sinking. I was already up to my waist in water. Then there was a power that lifted the canoe and carried it over the water and onto the land. What can that mean?"

I suggested that the dream was saying his "boat" was sinking—that is, he was about to fail in his pastorate—but a power would come to lift him and save his pastoral ministry. This is what happened to him at the conference.

*Your Dreams, God's Neglected Gift, Herman Riffel. Chosen Books, 1982.

Another pastor said he had dreamed he was trying to reach God but could not get to Him because there were some little men hindering him. He tried and tried, until finally there was a ladder set up for him to climb to God.

I asked the interpreter what the "little men" were. He said they might refer to pygmies. This, however, was a rational answer. It took a little time for us to learn what the "little men" really referred to. The answer came when I visited an African village in the forest. The chief met us where the path entered the village. He led us into a little tepee-like hut, explaining that when a villager died they would cut a stick, peel its bark, name the stick after the man, and place it inside the hut. These sticks he called "little men." Then, when the men went on a hunt, they made an offering and placed it at the door of the hut, thus to ensure success on their venture.

I could see that by making this offering they were worshiping the spirits of the dead. And then I could understand that the "little men" in the pastor's dream referred to their witchcraft, which occultist practice was hindering the pastor from coming to God. The other national pastors understood the meaning of the "little men," but I had to learn its meaning from them to understand what the dream was saying.

In the same dream a ladder was finally set up for this pastor by which he got to God. The ladder reminded him that there would be an access to heaven provided for him—which happened at the conference.

So his was an encouraging dream. It was also very personal, which is the nature of dreams. They speak personally to the dreamer, revealing his inner life and often giving promises concerning the future.

Daniel said to Nebuchadnezzar concerning his dream:

> As for you, O king, while on your bed your
> thoughts turned to what would take place in the
> future; and He who reveals mysteries has made
> known to you what will take place. But as for me,
> this mystery has not been revealed to me for any
> wisdom residing in me more than in any other
> living man, but for the purpose of making the
> interpretation known to the king, and that you
> may understand the thoughts of your [*heart*,
> which is a clearer translation than *mind*].
>
> (Daniel 2:29–30)

This statement of Daniel's contains some important
principles of dream interpretation. First, it suggests that
the dream reveals the thoughts of the heart, as over against
the thoughts of the mind. The thoughts of Nebuchadnezzar's mind were that he was greater than any man, even
the gods. The thoughts of his heart, revealed by the dream,
showed that he knew there was a God of mighty power,
even though he did not know Him personally.

Second, the dream often reveals what will happen if we
continue to go in the direction (inwardly) that we are
going. Nebuchadnezzar's dream, discerned by Daniel,
revealed the judgment of God coming upon him if he did
not change the direction of his heart's attitude. The dreams
of the two African pastors showed that if they went to the
conference as they planned, they would receive the help
they sought. So the dream may give us a promise that will
be fulfilled if we continue in the right way, or it may give us
a warning to correct our ways.

Third, Daniel's statement points out that dream interpretation is *revelation* for the purpose of understanding. As Daniel said, the king's dream and its interpretation were not given to him because he was an extraordinary person. Anyone may seek God's help in interpreting dreams who is willing to pay the price to learn as Daniel did.

It is important for us to realize, however, that we in Western culture have lost the basic understanding of dreams, which must be relearned. If, given that premise, we will submit ourselves to God, then He will teach us as He did Daniel. We must not presume that we know how to interpret dreams without careful study, any more than we would expect a doctor to know how to perform surgery without studying medicine. We must learn all we can and submit that learning to God and His Word.

Think of a dream as the mirror of the soul, reflecting what is going on within us. It reveals our "blind spots," things we do not see about ourselves but that others see in us. This is one reason a dream is often hard to understand. In fact, it is only when we are willing to see the truth about ourselves and to follow the dream's instructions that we will be able to understand it.

Dreams are like parables, which Jesus explained in this way:

> For whoever has, to him shall more be given, and he shall have an abundance; but whoever does not have, even what he has shall be taken away from him. Therefore I speak to them in parables; because while seeing they do not see, and while hearing they do not hear, nor do they understand.
>
> (Matthew 13:12–13)

One of the most common mistakes is to interpret a dream literally. When we dream about other people, we tend to assume the dream is speaking of them. Most often people in our dreams reflect a part of ourselves. We need to ask what those people represent to us and what we are doing in real life that they are doing symbolically in the dream.

When I dreamed of a boyhood friend I had not thought about for a long time, I considered what he represented to me. The impression that came was that, despite other good character qualities, he was the most dogmatic fellow I had ever met.

Surely I am not like that! I said to myself. Upon reflection, however, I realized that at the time I was dogmatically arguing a point with someone. My dream was saying, "This is what you look like"—not necessarily that I was a dogmatic person, but that I was acting like one.

Each of our dreams is like one frame in a movie film: it reveals a character trait at the immediate time of the dream. A series of dreams reveals more common characteristics of the personality.

We are told that ninety-five percent of our dreams are subjective—that is, they reflect ourselves. Only five percent are objective, meaning the dreams are actually saying something about the persons we are dreaming about. To find out whether a dream is objective or subjective, we should first "try it on," listening carefully to the Lord to see what the dream might be saying about ourselves. It may take days, even weeks, to get the meaning of a dream.

If, after considering it carefully, prayerfully, and with the help of others, it still does not "fit," then we may accept it as an objective dream about someone else. This does not mean we tell that person what we have dreamed. (We must be very careful how we handle our dreams.) Rather, the dream may be a call to prayer on behalf of that person.

We may wonder sometimes whether we can trust the interpretation of a dream, for it seems that one dream could have many and even opposite meanings. However, this is not the case. While the dream may have many levels of meaning—some superficial levels but with gradually deeper and deeper meanings—it still has the same basic message. Only the dreamer will recognize when the interpretation to his dream is correct.

This principle is clearly illustrated in the Bible. When the great Pharoah of Egypt had a dream that neither his magicians nor the wise men could interpret, a captive slave named Joseph interpreted it. Pharoah recognized it immediately as the correct interpretation and elevated Joseph to a position next to his throne. Similarly, when another captive slave, Daniel, interpreted Nebuchadnezzar's dream, the great monarch fell on his face, did homage to Daniel, and made him ruler over the whole province of Babylon, because he knew that interpretation was correct.

This illustrates what we often see when we help people understand their dreams. The dreamer recognizes when the interpretation is correct because it confirms what he knows, though he may not consciously be aware of it.

It is important that we do not accept an interpretation of a dream that our hearts do not confirm. Nor are we ever to force an interpretation of a dream upon the dreamer. We may suggest what it means but leave it with the dreamer to recognize if it is correct. In fact, I recommend that one has at least five years of experience evaluating his own dreams before beginning to interpret those of other people, although it is helpful to have someone with whom you can share your dreams and so learn from each other.

Perhaps you are protesting, "But I don't dream." We all dream; we simply may not remember our dreams, for several reasons. The most common is that we have been taught to ignore them. Another reason is that a dream evaporates when the mind becomes active (which is why a radio alarm is most detrimental to remembering dreams). It is a good idea to have pen and paper handy by your bed and ask God to remind you of your dreams. Then, upon awakening from a dream, write it down immediately. Do not try to interpret it until all the details are on paper.

If we really want to hear God speak, we must listen. Of course, we can shut God out for a time, until He breaks through in a nightmare. But it is far better to listen to the gentle suggestions each night.

It is at night when the mind is still that God shows us things we refuse to hear during our waking hours. He gives us a mirror for our soul, so that we can know what the thoughts of our hearts really are. He warns us so that we do not fall in the way, and He gives us great promises that we could never have imagined.

It is important, then, to listen to dreams, because they are an important way God speaks to us night after night.

8

How God Speaks Through Visions

One of our friends was overwhelmed with sorrow. She was sitting at her sewing machine weeping. Suddenly she sensed a presence in the room and looked up. There she saw the face of Jesus, filled with such love and tenderness that her sorrow fled away, and great peace filled her soul.

People sometimes ask, "Why did the Lord give this woman such a vision? Why did He not simply tell her that He loved her?"

I reply, "He has told her that many times. She has often read about God's gracious love in her Bible. She has also heard that God loved her through the teaching she's received. But at that point she was overwhelmed with sorrow."

It seemed to me that God was saying, "She knows that I love her. She has filled her mind with My Word, but her heart is overwhelmed right now, so I will *show* her My love."

This is the reason He may show us in a vision what our minds cannot comprehend.

Sometimes God puts us to sleep in order to show us what we need to see, just as He showed Abraham the promise of the future of His nation. The more rational person may *have* to go to sleep, so that in that unconscious state the mind will not interfere and the dream can speak. For another person the unconscious breaks through even when he or she is wide awake.

The extreme condition, when the unconscious takes control and the mind is no longer heard, should certainly be avoided. God wants to bring us into balance. We are not to allow the conscious to block out messages from the unconscious, nor are we to allow the unconscious to block out the conscious. We need both the conscious and the unconscious, the mind and the heart, to speak to us.

A vision is basically the same as a dream, except it comes while we are awake. Both come from the deep unconscious part of ourselves, and both are gifts of God in order to correct, warn, instruct, guide, or give a promise to us.

Our Christian neighbor, Julie, had this report: "I had become very good friends with John and Ann, who did not know the Lord. Then John became ill; the doctor diagnosed it as cancer and the prognosis was not good. One morning I woke very early and found thoughts pouring through me of things I needed to say to them. But the words were also coming in pictures, as though drawn on a legal pad in my mind. The first picture was of the doorway we walk through when Christ comes into our lives. It led to a big room. The next picture, a second door, stood between the room of life and the next room of death. I knew it was really the doorway into the light, beauty, and sunshine of being present with Jesus in a new life. It was a picture of joy and anticipation and fulfillment. I was aware that it made no difference if we walked quickly from the first door to the second, or whether we spent many years with Jesus in the first room of life. And I knew from all this that the Lord wanted to talk with John and Ann about both life and death, to free them from fear.

"So I went to them. I drew the pictures for them that I had been given, and shared the words of peace and joy that went with the pictures.

"We all three wept tears of joy as John and Ann said yes to Jesus' knock at the door of their hearts. They then moved through the months of struggle and surgeries with a strength and peace that was a miracle to all who knew them. John died and Ann now lives alone, but yet not alone. Jesus lives with her and has given her a peace and strength that everyone can see. And she still has the piece of paper with those pictures that the Lord showed me for her and John."

A vision may come in various forms. Sometimes God breaks through the conscious level and shows us something in our world that our eyes cannot see, as with the sorrowing mother at her sewing machine. Sometimes He shuts out all other physical reality for the moment to make the message clear. This is like watching a picture on a large screen. And sometimes He creates a mental picture.

The New Testament records many of these kinds of visions. Some of them show us wrong ideas or actions that are a result of prejudice or pride, such as with the apostle Peter. Although Peter was willing to lay down his life for Jesus Christ, he still had a "blind spot" about receiving Gentiles into the Church.

He had been told that the Church was to incorporate the Gentiles, but still could not conceive of the idea. God saw the sincerity of Peter's heart but also the prejudice of his mind, so He put him into a trance. In that condition Peter's mind would not interfere with the vision God gave him of the lowering of a sheet filled with all kinds of animals, reptiles, and birds, which He told Peter were edible. Because of that vision, the Gentiles were included in the Church by Peter and the apostles.

The Transfiguration, which Jesus calls a vision, may provide some explanation of this phenomenon. We can imagine that as Jesus was deeply moved about His coming rejection and death, He took three of His companions with Him to pray. As He prayed, the glory of God came upon Him, and Moses and Elijah appeared talking to Him. By means of a vision, the others were able to see them, just as the followers of Jesus saw the angels after His resurrection (see Luke 24:23). So a vision seems to remove a veil from our eyes.

We may remember from the Old Testament that Elisha's servant was afraid when he saw the armies of the enemy surround their little village of Dothan (see 2 Kings 6). When Elisha prayed that the servant's eyes would be opened, the servant saw the hills covered with horses and chariots of fire. The spiritual army was already there to win the victory, but he could not see it until his eyes were opened. Then he, like Elisha, could see the spiritual realm as well as the natural.

As I was traveling in Mexico a few years ago, a friend pointed out a mountain above a little town. He said that a group of Christians had been so persecuted in the town that they had built some huts up on the side of the mountain to live in. One evening when the pastor was away, his wife called the Christians together for prayer, for they were again being threatened by the townspeople.

The next morning as some of the Christians went down to the town, they were surprised to find the townspeople looking at them in awe. Upon inquiring, they learned that the night before, while the little group of Christians was praying, the men in the town had climbed the mountain, determined to burn down the huts of the believers. But on the way they met an army that so frightened them that they turned back.

It was not the Mexican army that they met. They met the army of the Lord surrounding His children while they prayed. God had opened their eyes and given them a vision of another reality they had not counted on, to keep them from their purpose.

Similar reports of whole units of armies seeing the same kind of vision have come from both World Wars.

We have sometimes accused people, even those in good mental health, of seeing things that were not there. But perhaps they were seeing things that our physical eyes could not see. If so, it is important that we all learn to interpret what is seen. The vision, like the dream, speaks in symbolic language. This is evident in Ezekiel's vision (see chapters 1, 8, and 37 in particular), and it is true of all the prophets of the Bible. When some people have tried to interpret the vision of the apostle John in Revelation literally (rather than symbolically), it has produced much confusion.

As with dreams, the one who has a vision will know when the interpretation is correct, so long as he is walking honestly and humbly before God. There is just one exception. When a person has a vision for a person he or she is praying for, then the interpretation belongs to the one being prayed for.

This was illustrated clearly to Lillie and me on another occasion when we were house-hunting. At this time Lillie was especially eager to find her own nest, since we had been without a house for a year while carrying on our traveling ministry.

One particular week I was teaching a series on prayer in a little Mennonite church in Ontario, Canada, which was seriously interested in learning more about the walk of faith. Lillie and I loved Ontario's rolling countryside with its farm settings. Often while driving, as we saw a house nestled against a clump of trees and bushes, one of us would say, "Wouldn't that be a nice setting for a home!"

That week a pastor friend from Michigan phoned us about a house he thought Lillie and I might be interested in. In fact, he offered to fly us to Michigan to see the house, then fly us back to Ontario for the remainder of the week of ministry. We were touched by his kindness, but uncertain as to God's leading in such a pressured situation.

That evening at the church, my subject was "Listening" as an important aspect of prayer. After giving the lecture, I asked the group of some fifty people to listen with Lillie and me to see whether we should take the pastor up on his kind offer to fly us to Michigan.

Overwhelmingly the words that came said for us to wait. The people had received statements like these: "In quietness and confidence shall be your strength." "The Son of man had not a place to lay His head." "Except the Lord build the house, they labor in vain who build it."

"My God shall supply all your needs." "God does not usually rush into things." "Simply trust Him day by day." The sum of their statements clearly confirmed to us that we were not to rush away to see the house.

Afterward, a mature Christian woman came to us and reported—a bit reluctantly—a vision she had received. "In my vision," she said, "I saw a huge green maple tree. It was so large that it completely filled my sight. I could not look around it. I tried and tried, but the tree was too large. Finally I did manage to look around it and saw the Lord behind the tree."

Since the maple tree might relate to the maple leaf of Canada, she suggested the vision might be saying that we should live in Canada. To be sure, Lillie and I would have liked nothing better. As soon as she told me the vision, however, I knew what it meant. I had the instant conviction that the Lord was also saying to Lillie and me, "Canada has so filled your vision that you cannot see the Lord anymore."

Because the people were praying for *us*, the interpretation of the vision belonged to me. And when the right house finally came along, Lillie and I knew we had heard God rightly.

Much hurt has been done to people when an interpretation of a dream or vision is pressed upon them, even though they do not feel that is the appropriate message. When we receive a vision for another, we may gently suggest what we have seen and ask the person whether it means anything to him or her. God will verify His message; we do not have to try to do it with our own "authority" or "wisdom."

When Louisa and Pat, two friends, work together as a prayer team, Louisa prays audibly and Pat prays silently. While doing so, Pat often finds that a picture will come to mind. She tries to dismiss it as a test to see if it is really valid. If it stays with her, she tells the one for whom they are praying—hesitantly at first—what she saw, and asks if it means anything to the person. Usually the person responds with "Oh yes, indeed."

One day Louisa and Pat were counseling a placid, mild-mannered woman who was apparently having a problem with her husband. As they prayed and waited on the Lord for this woman, Pat began to see a picture of a boat. In the picture the woman was having a hard time trying to put a motor in. The picture seemed so incongruous that Pat did not want to mention what she saw, but when the picture did not leave, she admitted she had seen a boat.

"Oh, I love boats," responded the woman immediately, to the surprise of Pat and Louisa.

Pat then told her about the motor that did not seem to fit into the boat. Then the woman admitted that this boat was used for her pleasure, and that the motor probably represented the contention over it with her husband. Not only was this a confirmation to Pat that what she had seen was really from the Lord, but by that one picture she and Louisa were able to see right into the heart of the woman's surprising problem with her husband.

We see, then, that a vision reveals things that cannot be seen with physical eyes, and often reveals truth that cannot be understood by the human mind. On the one hand we must acknowledge that a vision reveals a reality that is there. On the other hand, it is equally important to remember that a vision speaks in symbolic language and must be interpreted rightly. The laws of interpretation are the same as we have already described in the previous chapter on how God speaks through dreams.

Whenever God speaks by word or dream or vision, it is important to listen to what He is saying, learn to understand it, and then obey it.

9

How God Speaks
Through Prophecy

The gift of prophecy is described by the apostle Paul in his letter to the Corinthians like this: "One who prophesies speaks to men for edification and exhortation and consolation" (1 Corinthians 14:3). Or, from the NIV: "Everyone who prophesies speaks to men for their strengthening, encouragement and comfort."

This puts prophecy on a level we can all understand and participate in. It may come in preaching and teaching; it can also come in the unobtrusive ways that the Holy Spirit guides the Christian.

I now recognize that many years ago, when prophecy was not recognized in the church where I was a young pastor, this gift was nevertheless in operation. I faced occasional discouragement there on account of a deacon who seemed to question my every decision. But a gracious elderly man often came to our home on Monday mornings—the day a pastor usually needs encouragement.

"Pastor," he once said, "don't worry about Peter. I know he seems to be opposing you, but he does that to everyone, and he doesn't really mean it the way you take it."

"It certainly makes me question my own decisions," I responded.

"But that's good, so long as you don't allow it to discourage you. Do what you know is right and forget about the questionings."

Those few words of strengthening and comfort encouraged me greatly and helped me see things from a different perspective. Further, they were spoken wisely, lovingly, and with great blessing to the church. Neither he nor I, however, had any idea that the gift of prophecy was being exercised.

It is important to remember that the one speaking may not know he is giving a word of prophecy, but the hearer will know it. Some time ago I commented to a group of people that I had never given a word of prophecy. "Yes, you have," one replied. "That time you prayed for us was a prophecy to us, and furthermore, it has been fulfilled."

Most of us tend to think of prophecy as coming in fine authoritative tones. The authority in a word of prophecy, however, does not lie in the voice or eloquence of the speaker who intones *Thus saith the Lord!* The message can be given casually, even softly. But the authority becomes evident to the hearer who says in his own heart, "That was a word of the Lord for me."

The word of prophecy may come in very practical terms. Luke, the physician and historian, tells us that one of the members of the church in Jerusalem became aware by the Spirit that a famine was coming during the reign of Claudius. He went to the church in Antioch and told them of it. As a result, the church in Antioch was moved to take up an offering for the Christians in Jerusalem, which they sent by way of Saul and Barnabas (see Acts 11:27–30). So by a word of prophecy the church in Jerusalem was spared the ravages of a famine.

There is another way prophecy may become the channel for the voice of God—the way Paul exercised this gift with Timothy.

Paul had found Timothy, who was well spoken of by the Christians, while traveling through Lystra and Derbe on his second missionary journey. He wanted to bring Timothy with him. So in preparation, Paul and the elders of the church laid their hands on the young convert, whereupon God gave a word of prophecy, saying Timothy was receiving a spiritual gift.

Later, Paul wrote a letter to Timothy from his prison cell, calling on him not to "neglect the spiritual gift within you, which was bestowed upon you through prophetic utterance with the laying on of hands by the [elders]" (1 Timothy 4:14).

Still Timothy apparently did not exercise the gift he had received as Paul thought he should, so Paul wrote a second letter in which he said, "I remind you to kindle afresh the gift of God which is in you through the laying on of my hands" (2 Timothy 1:6).

This suggests that prophecy is not fulfilled automatically but operates on the principle laid down in the Old Testament:

> At one moment I might speak concerning a nation or concerning a kingdom to uproot, to pull down, or to destroy it; if that nation against which I have spoken turns from its evil, I will relent concerning the calamity I planned to bring on it.
>
> (Jeremiah 18:7–8)

If a warning had been given to a particular nation, judgment would come on it only if it did not repent of its sins. If it did repent, judgment would not fall.

The same principle applies to blessings:

> Or at another moment I might speak concerning a nation or concerning a kingdom to build up or to plant it; if it does evil in My sight by not obeying My voice, then I will think better of the good with which I had promised to bless it.
>
> (verses 9–10)

Lillie and I have seen this principle in action. There came a point in our ministry, while located in the suburbs of Detroit, when we did not know what lay ahead of us. I had been a pastor for twenty-five years. A chain of events indicated that this avenue was now closed. We needed a word from God for fresh direction. After considering carefully, we decided to ask for help.

Nearby was Bethesda Missionary Temple, which ministered to many churches and pastors in the area. When we discovered they prayed for people who were seeking direction, we asked the pastor to put our names on the list. Soon afterward, we were invited to come and receive prayer.

About a thousand people were in attendance at this weekday session. We were invited to come to the pulpit. The pastors and elders gathered around and prayed for us. Then they stopped to listen. Here are the words of prophecy we then received:

> The Lord hath spoken unto thee and He doth confirm it today that He hath caused thee to pull up thy stakes, and to reset thy stakes, and to

make the tent and the place of thy dwelling a
very, very large place. Yes, the Lord shall enlarge
the place of your dwellings. The Lord shall cause
thee to break forth on the right hand and on the
left hand and the Lord shall cause thee to walk by
many ways and many roads and beside many
waters. . . . Be strong in the Lord, for the Lord
thy God doth lay His hand upon thee and bind
thee together. He doth bind thee together as one.
Thy ministry shall be as one. . . . For the Lord
shall send thee forth as trumpets. . . . For the
Lord thy God shall be with thee and all resistance
shall be broken down whithersoever God doth
send thee, and thou shalt have harvest in many
places. . . . The Lord doth say unto thee, Look
not back on the past but look ye forward . . . for
the Lord doth change thy lives from this day
forward.

When we received this encouraging prophecy, the
pastors reminded us that these promises would not be
fulfilled automatically, but only if we believed the words
God had spoken and if we acted in obedience. For us, part
of that obedience was waiting for God's timing. It took a
year before it began to be fulfilled. But after twenty-five
years of a local pastorate, our ministry was to change
radically.

Within a year, invitations began to come from missionaries in nearly a dozen countries asking us to come and
minister to them. From then on invitations never ceased
coming. We have now visited more than forty countries in
the course of ministry that the Lord has given us.

Furthermore, though we have presented many new and challenging thoughts, God has overcome all resistance in every place He has sent us. We must only be obedient to go where the Lord sends us, and present the message He gives us.

You may have noticed that the prophecy was given to us in Elizabethan English. That did not make it any more authoritative than if it had been spoken in everyday American English. It just happened that the person who gave the prophecy commonly used the King James Version of the Bible, and when speaking in religious terms used that language.

The important thing is, a word of prophecy must be tested. It is much like rain. Rain comes from the sky in pure form, but as it falls though our atmosphere it mixes with our pollution and may even become acid rain. God's message issues from His mouth in pure form, but as it comes to us it mixes with our prejudice, fear, pride, and selfishness.

This is why Paul said, "Let two or three prophets speak, and let the others pass judgment" (1 Corinthians 14:29). We will describe this further in Chapter 15, "Testing What I Hear." None of us is fully mature, but we are all learning, and God is quite willing to correct and guide us gently.

We need to recognize, therefore, that God still speaks today through prophecy, which may come from any sincere Christian in a word of encouragement to another. It need not be spoken in a church or uttered in "religious" tones to be a legitimate word from God; it need only be directed by the Holy Spirit.

But even if offered by a recognized prophet, it still is not for condemnation but for the "strengthening, encouragement and consolation" of the Church.

10 How God Speaks through A Word of Wisdom or Knowledge

Ann keeps busy directing a home of twenty-five to thirty troubled girls. She deals with many crisis situations in her work, and says that sometimes an idea just comes to her, giving her special insight into a particular situation.

"One day, for instance," she told me, "Sue and Linn came in battling. They sat down opposite each other in lounge chairs, ready to kill one another verbally. The first thing God said to me was, *The issue has nothing to do with what they are saying. Give Sue your attention.*

"So I turned to Sue and said, 'How are you feeling?'

"She was incredulous, as if to say, 'What does that have to do with our fight?'

"But God had directed me to Sue's feelings, so I pursued it. 'What is it that's really hurting you?'

"That question was like a pin puncturing a balloon, and Sue burst into tears. Then she told me things were not going well in school, which is where she got her mother's approval. Even when she told me things she was doing that were wrong, the Lord directed me to say, 'How can I help you with the pain you are feeling?' Sue melted, and I was awed at how God worked. Even Linn melted and asked how she could help."

For Ann, the voice of God provided insights that cut through confusion and secondary issues and got right to the heart of the issue.

The word of wisdom and the word of knowledge are gifts or manifestations of the Holy Spirit in the lives of believers. Jesus said, "You shall receive power when the Holy Spirit has come upon you; and you shall be My witnesses" (Acts 1:8). The Church did receive power to witness when the Holy Spirit came. In fact, that power was so great that through Peter's preaching some three thousand people received Christ and were baptized in a single day.

The Western Church has not put much emphasis on the gifts of the Holy Spirit until recently, but even so, these gifts are not altogether strange to us. Despite the fact that we have not often identified them, we may yet have some familiarity with them. We have doubtless received special wisdom from God that solved a difficult problem—such as the time in my pastorate when my older friend offered such encouragement. Or we may know of a mature Christian telling a younger man or woman with conviction that he is called to a specific work. Perhaps we have received such a word ourselves and have seen it come to pass.

Jimmy Smith, who has a ministry of music combined with other spiritual gifts, offers this definition: "A word of wisdom gives instruction or direction. A word of knowledge gives partial information, though it does not show the whole picture. It may come as a vision or a word. It can also trigger prophecy."

There is a twofold value in identifying a word of wisdom and a word of knowledge: First, Christians can then seek and expect that the gifts of the Holy Spirit will be given;

and second, when they are given, they will be recognized as gifts from God and received with appropriate gratitude. The gifts of the Spirit, listed in 1 Corinthians 12, are not defined there. But we see them illustrated in the life of Jesus in the Gospels and in the history of the Church in Luke's record in the book of Acts, so we will draw our illustrations from these records.

Jesus promised a gift of wisdom with this statement:

> Behold, I send you out as sheep in the midst of wolves. . . . They will deliver you up to the courts . . . [but] do not become anxious about how or what you will speak; for it shall be given you in that hour what you are to speak. For it is not you who speak, but it is the Spirit of your Father who speaks in you.
>
> (Matthew 10:16–20)

Evidently Jesus Himself experienced this phenomenon when He was opposed by the Jewish leaders and they sent officers to take Him. When the officers returned without Him, the chief priests and Pharisees asked, "Why did you not bring Him?" The officers replied, "Never did a man speak the way this man speaks."

We see the gift of wisdom also illustrated in the experience of Stephen, one of the seven chosen to help widows in the early Church. As Stephen began to work miracles and signs by the Holy Spirit, he was challenged by members of the synagogue. Stephen was not trained in the Law as they were, and was no match for them, but he was filled with the Holy Spirit.

So, just as Jesus promised for the time of trial, Stephen

was given words of wisdom by God the Holy Spirit, so that "they were unable to cope with the wisdom and the Spirit with which he was speaking" (Acts 6:10). This frustrated them so much that they stoned him and made him the first martyr of the Church. Stephen's death led to the salvation of Paul, and the great missionary ministry that followed. And out of it came the saying, "The blood of the martyrs is the seed of the Church."

At a crisis point in my own ministry, I discovered firsthand that the gift of wisdom is still available. I had learned years before how to find the proper text or subject for my speaking appointments, while I knew from experience the vital difference between a sermon (a compilation of selected material) and a genuine message from God (when the minister has sought God's guidance for the occasion). At this particular time, when my faith in the validity of the Scriptures was being challenged, a strange thing happened.

I received neither a Scripture text nor a sermon subject for the upcoming Sunday service, though I sought them earnestly. I grew desperate, knowing that my own store of wisdom in choosing sermon material for such a time would not be sufficient. Then, on Saturday night, the Lord reminded me of His instruction that when we are on trial, we are not to prepare our words, for He will give us words to say. (See Matthew 10:16–20.)

After much wrestling over the problem, I went to bed. It was with trembling that I walked into the church that Sunday morning, not knowing what I was to speak about. We began the service as usual. Not even Lillie knew what was going on in my mind. We sang the hymns and received the offering and the choir sang in praise of God, and still I did not receive a hint from the Lord about the sermon.

The time came. I got up and started toward the pulpit. Then, to my surprise, thoughts came tumbling into my mind. I preached and the words poured out until the sermon time was over.

The same thing happened that evening, and again the next Sunday, and the next. The freedom and power of the Holy Spirit accompanied my ministry during two full months of crisis in the church. I knew this kind of preaching lay beyond my potential or experience. The Holy Spirit was evidently giving me the word of wisdom for that time of trial.

Those parishioners, eager to receive God's Word, told me I had never preached with such freedom and power. Those who were resisting the Holy Spirit, on the other hand, felt deeply threatened. It precipitated a crisis in the church that ended in my sudden dismissal. God was closing down one phase of my life and opening a new world to Lillie and me. He then sent us out on the ministry that has taken us around the world, and has resulted in twenty years of traveling ministry.

Thus, while I believe in the importance of preparation, I know there are times the Lord will not allow me to prepare an outline or even a note for a certain speech or conference, because He has something special to give me for that occasion.

Sometimes in an emergency we have no time to prepare, but need an answer from God immediately. In Ann's case, working with troubled young girls, the voice of God comes through ideas. She recognizes them confidently because they have proven to contain the insight she needs in her ministry. "When these thoughts come," she says, "I have such assurance that God is speaking to me that I act quickly. I've made mistakes, of course, but I usually realize they are mistakes. Then I acknowledge it and try to make things right."

The word of wisdom may come to a mother who does not know which way to turn at a critical point in the training of her children, or to a young man as he stands for his faith among unbelievers, or to an executive in an office who has an important decision to make. We need only have a clean and open heart before God to receive the wisdom He has to give.

Similar to the word of wisdom, but perhaps a bit more specific, is the word of knowledge. This gift must have been given to Peter as he led that thrilling "testimony meeting" described by Luke in Acts 4:32–5:11, which turned out to be a terrible manifestation of the power of God.

Barnabas had just brought the money from the sale of his estate and laid it at the apostles' feet. Ananias apparently did the same. But the apostle Peter received a sudden insight or word of knowledge concerning Ananias' deceit and challenged him about lying to God.

What disruption and trouble it would have caused if God had not been behind Peter's challenge! But Peter believed the word of knowledge that he had received and spoke it under the direction of the Spirit. God immediately gave proof that the word received by Peter *was* of Him, when Ananias died a very sudden death.

It happened as a judgment of God upon the man, but the higher purpose was to preserve the Church in its purity. And afterward "all the more believers in the Lord, multitudes of men and women, were constantly added to their number" (Acts 5:14).

Let us see how the word of knowledge may come today and compare it with the scriptural records. I was addressing doctors and medical professionals on board the Youth With A Mission ship, the *Anastasis*, off the coast of New Zealand. As I spoke of the practicality of faith in medicine, Dr. Peter Voss, secretary of the Christian Medical Fellowship, offered an illustration.

"As I was diagnosing the ailments of a patient," he said, "certain pictures began to come to me. At first I didn't know what to do with them. Then I ventured to ask my patient if the pictures meant anything to him. I was surprised to find that they were very meaningful, for they either described his condition or brought back memories. When this happened more than once, I learned that these pictures were not just my imagination. God was giving me specific help in diagnosing the physical condition of my patients. Now I know this is the word of knowledge given by means of pictures or visions."

Another way the word of knowledge may come was described by Curry Vaughn, pastor of the Tabernacle Church in Melbourne, Florida. "One day I was talking to a young woman," he told me. "From a strong impression inside of me, I said, 'I feel that something terrible happened to you regarding your father. I see the place where it happened as a cave.' While we were praying she started to weep. Then she said, 'My father took me into the shower one day and molested me. The shower stall was unfinished and looked like a cave.'"

It was clear that God had given Curry a word of knowledge concerning that woman, which opened the way for her healing.

Jesus Himself was often the recipient of special knowledge that enabled him to minister or direct His disciples in a most specific way. Before His triumphal entrance into Jerusalem, He told them:

> "Behold, when you have entered the city, a man will meet you carrying a pitcher of water; follow him into the house that he enters. And you shall say to the owner of the house . . . 'Where is the guest room in which [the Teacher and His disciples] may eat the Passover . . . ?' And he will show you a large, furnished, upper room; prepare it there." . . . And they departed and found everything just as He had told them.
>
> (Luke 22:10–13)

How did Jesus know those things? On other occasions— such as the time He did not seem to know the fig tree was barren until He drew close (see Matthew 21:19)—Jesus did not seem privy to special knowledge at all. At other times, however, Jesus received supernatural insight from His heavenly Father.

Similar insight is recounted by evangelist Tommy Tyson. While he was preaching in a little country church years ago, the pastor requested that he accompany him on a visit to one of the families that had not attended church for a long time. As they approached the house, they saw the elderly couple sitting on the porch. Tommy noticed that the wife's arm seemed paralyzed.

After exchanging friendly conversation, Tommy received a word of knowledge in the form of two brief visions. In the first he saw a young man and woman racing off in a horse-drawn carriage, and he assumed they were that man and woman eloping. Then he saw the woman at an organ, deeply engrossed in her music. It seemed to him that the marriage had not been a happy one and that she had now lost herself in her music.

On the basis of these mental pictures, Tommy said boldly to the wife: "You eloped with this man against your parents' wishes and married him. Then he turned out to be a good-for-nothing husband. Isn't that right?"

"Yes," she said, "That *is* right, but—"

"Then, when your life was miserable with him, you poured out your soul playing the organ."

"Yes," she said, "that's right, too. But let me tell you the whole story. I did elope with this man and he turned out to be a good-for-nothing, as my parents had predicted. And I did pour out my soul in music on the organ. But later my husband turned into a good and loving man. Meanwhile, I became the organist at this little country church, where the former organist grew jealous of me and threatened to leave the church. Since she came from a large family who all attended the little church, and if she left the rest of the family would leave, too, my husband and I decided to withdraw. That's why we haven't attended the church for many years."

"And when you withdrew from the church your arm became paralyzed?" Tommy asked.

"Yes. That's when my arm got to be the way you see it now."

After explaining to her how the love of Christ heals all wounds, Tommy asked, "Would you be willing to forgive that woman and come to church next Sunday?"

"Yes," she said. "There's been too much time lost already."

As Tommy reached out his hand to say good-bye to her, her paralyzed arm was loosened and she reached out to him in response. Because Tommy had trusted God concerning the pictures he had been given, a great healing had taken place as that woman offered and received forgiveness.

Human wisdom is not sufficient to pierce the hard heart or the closed mind, but the words of wisdom and knowledge given by the Holy Spirit have heavenly powers. When Jesus told His followers not to leave Jerusalem until they received power from on high, it was because He knew they could not win the battle without special equipment. Paul described this equipment like this:

> For though we walk in the flesh, we do not war according to the flesh, for the weapons of our warfare are not of the flesh, but divinely powerful for the destruction of fortresses. We are destroying speculations and every lofty thing raised up against the knowledge of God, and we are taking every thought captive to the obedience of Christ.
>
> (2 Corinthians 10:3–5)

God speaks in power through the special equipment of the words of wisdom and knowledge. As we open our lives to the Holy Spirit, these gifts become available, but they become operable only as we act in obedience.

11

How God Speaks
In the Ministry of Healing

The telephone rang and I heard an anxious voice: "Will you come to the hospital? Our child is very sick!"

It was the voice of a young man whose wife I had visited when her son David was born six weeks before. Now she was in the hospital with him again. Of course I would come.

But before I could hang up the receiver I heard another voice: *Lay your hands on the child and I will heal him.* Never had I heard that before, yet the voice within my heart was as clear as any voice I had ever heard with my ears.

At that time I was just beginning to learn that God wanted to use His people in healing in this day. I had heard Dr. Albert Heustis, Health Commissioner for the state of Michigan for twenty years, express his view that the Church was neglecting the ministry of healing. There were aspects of sickness, he said, that medicine could not reach, that could be reached only through prayer. And he demonstrated it by laying his hands on the sick and praying for them.

For years I had resisted that kind of teaching. According to my training, healing was left to the doctors. Yet at this time many things in my life were changing and I knew God was dealing with me.

To obey the voice, which I knew was God's, would mean stepping into another theological realm. It could be costly since neither the local church nor my denomination was ready to receive a ministry of healing. On the other hand, I had exhausted all the resources of my training, and still there were needs I could not meet.

"Lord," I said, "I am not in the healing business." (As if He did not know!) And I went to the hospital with great trepidation.

Nevertheless, upon my arrival I simply told the anxious parents, "I believe God has given us a promise concerning your son. Let's ask Him for a healing and then thank Him." They seemed to receive these words with a joy and faith beyond my expectations.

Six-week-old David was under an oxygen mask. After the nurse gave me a gown to put over my clothes, I reached in, put my hand on his chest, and prayed a brief prayer for Jesus to touch him in healing. Then we thanked God, the parents were much encouraged, and I left the hospital.

A half-hour later the father called again. "David is much worse," he exclaimed.

I did not give voice to my own deeply anxious thoughts. "Let us continue to thank God," I responded, still convinced it was God's voice I had heard.

The parents seemed to accept this advice, and after two hours called again with good news: "David is much better." What a relief!

The baby remained sick for two more weeks, then recovered quickly. The specialist explained that there had been congestion of the lungs upon the heart, and the heart had stopped momentarily, but that a change had occurred and the child began to improve.

"How do you account for the change?" asked his parents.

"We can't really account for it. It just happened."

Along with David's parents and friends, we thanked God for the healing. The voice of God to me had apparently been the channel God used to heal that baby. I suspected His voice may have come many times before, but my ears had been dull of hearing through unbelief. Once they began to open, however, I was able to hear amazing things that I hardly dared to believe.

The voice of God is vitally important in the ministry of healing. We cannot take up a full study of healing in this book, of course, but we need to observe how important it was in the ministry of Jesus.*

In the early Scriptures we find certain basic principles of healing. God had said to Israel:

> If you will give earnest heed to the voice of the
> Lord your God, and do what is right in His sight,
> and give ear to His commandments, and keep all
> His statutes, I will put none of the diseases on
> you which I have put on the Egyptians; for I, the
> Lord, am your healer.
>
> (Exodus 15:26)

Much later the psalmist spoke of the Lord "who heals all your diseases" (Psalm 103:3).

Jesus commanded His disciples as follows: "Heal the sick, raise the dead, cleanse the lepers, cast out demons;

---

*For a fuller study of healing through prayer, see *Christian Maturity and the Spirit's Power*.

freely you have received, freely give" (Matthew 10:8). As He was preparing to leave this earth, Jesus said to His followers: "Truly, truly, I say unto you, he who believes in Me, the works that I do shall he do also; and greater works than these shall he do; because I go to the Father" (John 14:12).

From these basic principles, briefly given but abundantly demonstrated in the Scriptures, I have become convinced God wants to heal. He is a saving and healing God. In fact, the word used in the New Testament sometimes translated *saved* is at other times translated *healed* (compare John 3:17 and Mark 5:23). We must take the same attitude toward sickness that Jesus did. He always regarded sickness as an enemy (just as doctors do).

When we know the basic principles of healing, we can then move on for specific direction. To know that God heals is a basic principle but it does not give me healing, any more than my knowledge that a bank loans money guarantees that I will receive it. To do that, I must make application under specific regulations and meet the conditions.

In order to cooperate with God's healing plan, we must be in harmony with His purpose. So long as I did not believe God wanted to use me in the healing process, He could not get my attention. He could not tell me what He wanted me to do. Often our ears cannot hear what we do not want to hear.

We need God's direction in healing because the general word of Scripture must become the specific word for the occasion. The general word of the Law to Israel, for example, was that if they failed to obey God, He would withhold rain from the land and make the heavens as brass and the land as iron to them (Deuteronomy 28:15, 24–25). Israel failed to obey God, however, and the rain continued to fall. Then a specific word came to Elijah to put that warning to Israel into effect. When he obeyed the specific word that came to him, Elijah was given power to withhold the rain for three years, then call for it again.

Another general word from Scripture is that God wants to heal. But we need the specific word from the Holy Spirit today that will tell us how He wants to use us in the healing process.

Does He want to use me in the case of the arthritic woman before me, or is someone else better qualified to minister to her? Does he want me to focus my attention first on her physical needs, and then the rest of the person, as Jesus often did for people who came to Him? Does He want to begin with forgiveness, as He did with the paralytic (Matthew 9:1–8)?

Jesus was careful to do only what He saw the Father doing, and thus kept in perfect harmony with Him. So we must listen to hear what God wants to do through us, and how He wants to do it.

Another reason it is imperative to hear God's voice in the healing ministry is that through it, faith for the healing comes. St. Paul said, "Faith comes from hearing, and hearing by the word of Christ" (Romans 10:17). Often we do not know how to pray for the sick until we hear God tell us. Then, as the direction becomes specific, our faith rises too.

When I arrived back in Quito, Ecuador, after having been chaplain for the staff of the radio and television station HCJB, a couple met me at the plane. They asked if I would come and pray for their young adult daughter. She had been sick for some time; apparently prayers for her health were not being answered. I did not understand just what the problem was, but I was glad to come.

At their house a twenty-year-old woman lay in bed.

"Betsy, do you believe that if I prayed for you, you would be healed?" I asked her.

"I don't know," she answered. "So many people have prayed for me, yet I don't seem to get well."

Apparently she wanted to believe, but there had been too many disappointments already for faith to arise.

"I have to confess I can't believe it either," I said. "What are some of your smaller problems?"

"I can't sleep at night."

"Do you think God wants to give you a good night's sleep?"

"Yes, I do."

"Can you believe God will do it?"

"Yes," she said, "I can."

"I can, too," I replied.

It seemed that my faith should have been much bigger, but at least I knew I could believe God for a good night's sleep, and felt an inward nudging in that direction. So I prayed for Betsy, and the next morning when I stopped by she looked cheerful and felt better.

I left Ecuador soon afterward, and received reports after that that Betsy was still sick. I also learned she had a fatal disease called periarteritis for which the doctors had not yet found a cure.

Some years later Lillie and I were visiting her parents,

who now lived in the Boston area. We asked about Betsy's illness.

"Didn't you know Betsy was healed the night you prayed for her?" asked her mother.

"No," I said. "I heard she was sick for several years after our prayer."

"Oh, no," she said. "Betsy seemed to remain sick for eight months after you prayed for her. At that point the doctor checked her again and took her off the cortisone she had been taking. Immediately she got well. Apparently she had been healed of her sickness the night you prayed for her, but the cortisone had continued to make her sick."

I still do not believe it was my place to advise Betsy to go off the medication the doctor had prescribed for her, though I wish I had suggested they tell the doctor about the prayer and have him check her again.

I also realize that if I had tried to force myself to believe that God could heal her by my one prayer, it would have been presumption, not faith. Instead, I followed that inner voice, and was directed to a simple prayer for a good night's sleep. My faith could rise to that, and God could use it because it was real.

I also remembered that Jesus said, "If you have faith as a mustard seed, you shall say to this mountain, 'Move from here to there', and it shall move; and nothing shall be impossible to you" (Matthew 17:20). And I began to learn to pray in the way that God directs, whether it seemed great or small.

Jesus healed in many ways, and if we are followers of Him we must learn from Him. He commonly laid hands on the sick one by one. He sometimes touched people and they were healed. He spoke the word to the centurion who believed the word and his son was healed. In the case of Peter's mother-in-law, Jesus rebuked the fever and it left her. Sometimes people touched *Him* and were healed.

There were also times Jesus used physical means for healing. For the blind man he made clay, applied it to his eyes, and told him to go to the pool and wash, and as he did so, he was able to see. He also anointed with oil for healing, as James instructed the Church to do.

The doctor can be part of the healing team, too. We must listen to hear how God wants to heal the sick person. Are we to believe God and do nothing more? Are we to speak about it or keep still? Are we to send the sick one to the doctor? What kind of doctor? God has many ways of healing; we must listen to His direction and not let prejudice hinder us from any means that He wants to use.

In one case I learned about a boy in Michigan at a track practice kicked up a wood chip inadvertently at his ten-year-old schoolmate Eric, who fell to the ground. The teacher, seeing that Eric's eye was bleeding and part of the retina was detached, started praying immediately. She rushed him to the washroom, called his mother, and then God directed her to call an ophthalmologist.

The doctor said Eric could lose his eye and suggested an immediate operation, so Eric's mother, Margie, called her husband. She also called the church secretary, who notified friends to pray. The local doctor suggested that Margie and her husband, Joe, take Eric to the University of Michigan Kellogg Eye Center in Ann Arbor.

The doctors there said that although the condition was serious, they could not yet tell if they would have to take the lens out. That night they operated and stitched up the cornea, but did not remove the lens. They tried to sweep the iris into place but part of it had been lost. Now the parents were told to wait.

While praying, Margie had a vision in which she saw the Lord leaning over the operating table blowing life into Eric's eye. She was encouraged by this to believe that God was healing her son. Over the next four days there was a little bleeding. The eye pressure was dangerously low. So she and Joe prayed that the eye would stop bleeding and that the pressure in Eric's eye would increase.

Then Joe, who was not one to remember his dreams, had a vivid dream. In it he was up to bat in a baseball game, and wanted badly to hit a home run. But he could make only a base hit, then move one base at a time till he made it to home base. When he woke up, the Lord interpreted the dream for him. He assured Joe that, though He knew Joe wanted his son's healing to take place all at once, it was going to be a process and the healing would come one step at a time.

On the ninth day of Eric's hospitalization, his younger sister, Christy, awakened with the word *Bethsaida* on her mind. Joe and Margie looked up the reference in Mark 8:22–25, where Jesus laid His hands upon the blind man twice before he was healed. It was to be a *process* of healing, confirming Joe's dream. The whole family was encouraged. The next day Eric was released from the hospital, and after a few months his vision had returned to almost normal.

God had spoken through a mother's vision, a father's dream, and a little sister's word, and He had worked through the hands of doctors.

Sometimes our prayers for healing are not answered and we wonder why. There are many reasons, some beyond our understanding. As we listen to God, however, we find that He does want to hear our prayers and will often show us what the problem is.

Sometimes there are barriers that need to be removed. Gary and Linda Wilson had prayed and prayed for their little son, Daren. Many of their friends were praying, too, but Daren got worse instead of better. One day Gary felt the Lord telling him to surrender his little boy completely to Him. He did so, and immediately a word came in return: *From this time your child will get well.*

When Gary finally heard what the Lord was asking of him and did it, Daren began to improve until he got completely well.

Sometimes there are problems from childhood that need to be resolved with prayer for inner healing. While in Columbia, South America, I was conducting a seminar in which a pastor asked me to pray for his wife who had eczema all over her body. As soon as I prayed for her, the eczema left. But the next day it came back again. We prayed and it left again, only to return later.

Meanwhile, I sensed God leading me to speak on the subject of people's involvement in prayer for healing (James 5) at the little storefront church of the pastor. Much of the congregation, along with the elders, gathered at the pastor's house where his wife was again confined with the eczema. When I asked about her childhood, she told of being an orphan and sent from home to home. We prayed for healing of these hurts and again she responded beautifully.

It was still not all resolved, however. I learned after I left the country that when the missionary women gathered with her, she confessed she had slandered others in the village. Now they had reached the root of her problem. When they prayed for the eczema to leave, it did so for good.

When we know how responsive our skin is to our emotions, we should not be surprised at how something like eczema can come and go. The Lord wants us to get at the root of the symptoms and heal the cause of the sickness.

Sometimes when healing does not come, the Spirit of God may simply tell us to keep on praying. Charlotte's husband was an Air Force officer. Their son, Kirk, had a chronic blood condition. Each time a certain medication was reduced, his platelet count would fall off, until now the doctors were ready to remove his spleen. Charlotte and her parents had prayed and prayed, seemingly to no effect.

Then one morning while she was doing laundry, she felt strongly impressed once again to pray for Kirk. They had already prayed so often! That afternoon, when the impression was stronger than ever, she stopped hanging up the wash and rounded up her mother, who joined her readily in prayer. In Kirk's next weekly visit to the doctor, they learned there had been an improvement in his condition. And this time when the doctor reduced his medication, the platelet level remained constant. And eventually he was restored to health.

Charlotte knew she had heard the voice of God encouraging her to pray again, reminding her personally of what Jesus told His disciples: ". . . That at all times they ought to pray and not to lose heart" (Luke 18:1).

All these examples point up how important it is to receive the specific direction of the Lord for the ministry of healing. We must first be deeply convinced that God wants to heal. Then we need to find out whether God wants to use *us* in that healing. We remember that Jesus healed all that came to him, as Matthew tells us, but at the pool of Bethesda He healed only one man among a multitude of sick people (John 5:1–9).

Just as Jesus listened constantly to the Father and healed as He directed, so we must listen to Jesus as He directs us by His Holy Spirit in unique and original ways.

12

How God Speaks Through Angels

One of the special ways God speaks to man is through angels.

On several occasions God spoke in this way to Abraham. We have already alluded to the time Abraham was sitting at his tent door and saw three men approaching. He must have sensed something unusual about them, for he ran to meet them, bowing low and offering to serve them. After showing them hospitality, Abraham was given surprising news: that Sarah would conceive a child. The men also had to reprove Sarah, who laughed at the notion that she at the age of ninety should bear a child.

One of the "men" in that episode turned out to be the Lord in human form, and the other two, angels who went on to rescue Lot from the destruction of Sodom.

It seems from the Scriptures that angels often appear in human form and fit into the surroundings. When the angel Gabriel suddenly stood at the right side of the altar of incense in the Temple, the priest Zacharias was awe-struck and terribly frightened. That mighty angel of God must have appeared to him in all his glory and might.

When the same mighty angel entered the common home of the virgin Mary in the village of Nazareth, it does not seem that he appeared in the same way. Probably he did not need to impress her as he did the priest, since she was apparently more amazed at his words than at his appearance.

Dr. V. Raymond Edman, former president of Wheaton (Illinois) College, told of an experience he and Mrs. Edman had as young missionaries in Ecuador. They were working among the Quichua Indians of that country, where the farmers built mud walls on their boundaries instead of fences, for economic reasons. Driving through the countryside, you hardly saw any land from one house to the next, since the houses on both sides of the road were joined by solid mud walls for miles on end.

On this particular occasion, Dr. Edman and his young wife were very discouraged. Despite their hard work and fervent prayer for the Indians, their work did not seem to be taking effect. One day an Indian woman, dressed in the long dress and black felt hat typical of Quichua women, appeared at their door. She would not step inside but spoke in a most encouraging way of the Edmans' ministry in Ecuador. Amazed and impressed by the spiritual encouragement she offered, Dr. Edman turned to speak to his wife, whereupon Mrs. Edman urged him to invite her inside. But when he turned back to the door, no one was there. He looked down the road as far as he could see, but it was empty.

He was even more amazed than before, for no one could have run from his sight or escaped over the wall, particularly not a Quichua woman in long dress. As Dr. Edman considered this matter, he remembered the unusual and inspiring words she had spoken, and he and his wife concluded that God must have sent an angel in the form of a Quichua woman to encourage them.

Such experiences are hard for many in our Western culture to accept, bound as we are by the limitations of reason and our five senses. But consider the many astonishing biblical accounts of angelic visitation. The angels ministered to Jesus after the temptation and His forty-day fast. An angel opened the prison door for the disciples, and later for Peter, despite four squads of soldiers guarding him. An angel guided Philip to the Ethiopian treasurer; suggested to Cornelius, the Roman officer, to call for Peter to show him the way of salvation; and stood by Paul in the shipwreck.

It may be less surprising, in light of the numerous scriptural references to angels, to accept the experience of a Russian soldier in recent times, and see how it compares with the experiences we read about in Scripture. In her book *Vanya* , Myrna Grant tells how Ivan tried hard to live a Christian life in the Soviet army in 1971. When other soldiers asked him questions about his faith, he answered them honestly. When the officers tried to silence him and found they could not, they would beat him, jail him, or put him out in the snow for hours at a time. Note how God encouraged him one night:

"Although regulation bunk beds were only two feet wide and hard, Ivan stretched out between the sheets and beneath a blanket and thanked God for the luxury. For the first time in 1971 he was in bed. No hours in the cold. No interrogations in the snow or in the officers' rooms. No watching the moon set behind the tiny park in the central square. Even before taps were sounded, Ivan was blissfully asleep.

"Although he had only heard it once before, the Voice was so familiar, Ivan was instantly awake. 'Vanya, arise!' In a second he was on his feet between the bunks gazing at the crystal brilliance of the angel. His mind was working rapidly. He was aware that no sleeping soldier in the rows of bunks stirred. Mechanically he began to pull on his trousers and feel for his shoes, his eyes never leaving the radiant loveliness of the being before him. The angel's gaze was so full of love he felt no fear. In an instant they both began to rise, and effortlessly the ceiling opened and then the barracks' roof, and Ivan and the angel flew through time and space to another world.

"The grass was deep and lush and seemed to stretch to the very horizon of this unfamiliar planet. It was a fresh and vivid green. Dazed, Ivan followed the angel, and after what seemed to be a long time they came to a brook. Its waters were as clear as glass so Ivan could see the bed of the stream, and the brightness of the water dazzled his eyes. . . .

"In the brilliance of this world, every detail of blade of grass and petal of flower stood out as if floodlit. . . . The expanse of the branches were profoundly graceful, so luminous that the light seemed to pour from within each tree. Instinctively, Ivan lifted his eyes to the sky, gazing in every direction. There was no sun.

"When his eyes returned to the angel, there was a form beside the being, more exalted and at the same time somehow more loving in his brilliance than even the angel. In some way the angel seemed to do him deference, and Ivan knew him to be the apostle John. Through the angel, the apostle communicated with him. Ivan stood transfixed, his mind absorbing every holy word. A series of three beings followed the apostle, recognized in some mysterious way by Ivan to be David, Moses, and Daniel. So intense was Ivan's concentration and so overwhelming his awe and joy that when the last form was gone Ivan felt he would fall into a deep sleep. But the angel, now alone in the streaming light, spoke again.

" 'We have traveled a long way and you are tired. Come and sit.'

"The tree under which Ivan sat was large and welcoming, with a fragrance that reminded him in some unexplained way of the grape fields of Moldavia. If the angel had not spoken again Ivan felt he would be content to sit forever, smelling the tree and looking at the landscape in the sparkling light.

" 'I wish to show you the heavenly city, the new Jerusalem, but if you see it as it is, you cannot remain in the body you now have. And there is still much work for you left on earth.' There seemed a silence before the angel resumed speaking. 'We will fly together to another planet and I will show you the light of this city for you to know, while you are yet alive in your earthly body, that in certainty there is a new Jerusalem.'

"No man rescued from a desert ever drank water more thirstily than Ivan drank in the splendor of that light. So great was its power, it could be felt, tasted, heard. The sight of it was not a sensation of his eyes, but of his whole heart and being. Ivan could have wept with grief and disappointment when the angel said, 'The time has come to fly back to earth.'

"At the instant that Ivan's feet touched the floor beside

his bunk, three things happened. The angel disappeared, the bugle for reveille sounded, and the lights in the room snapped on. Staring stupidly at his neat bed and himself fully dressed, Ivan heard a gentle laugh from the bunk beside him. Grigorii Fedorovich Chernykh, his neighbor, was also a Moldavian and took fraternal interest in his strange countryman. Now Chernykh was pulling himself expertly out of his bunk and shoving his feet into trouser legs as he whispered in a conspiratorial tone, 'Vanya, where were you last night?'

"With a tremendous effort Ivan pulled his thoughts together. The barracks was alive with bodies hurling past his bunk to the door. Good-natured bantering, the groaning of exhausted soldiers, the flash of uniforms seemed unreal. He turned to look intently at Chernykh.

" 'You don't mean that you didn't see me getting undressed and into bed last night? We turned in at the same time.'

Chernykh was buttoning his shirt rapidly. 'You went to bed the same time I did, all right, and to sleep, too. But you didn't sleep long. I woke up about three A.M. and your bunk was empty. Vanya, you were nowhere in the room.' Reaching for his jacket, he gave Ivan a sly smile. 'Of all people, did you actually go A.W.O.L. last night?'

"He had not been dreaming! He had journeyed with the angel! Excitement tore through Ivan like electricity. They were moving hurriedly to the door.

"His voice shook as he spoke. 'Let's ask the duty officer if anyone left during the night.'

"The duty officer was indignant. 'Certainly no one left the room. Get going! Are you trying to get me arrested?!'

"Ivan and Grigorii Chernykh moved out into the morning, both in silence. Finally Chernykh broke the spell of strangeness with a question and Ivan began to tell him about the angel."*

Ivan's amazing experience may be hard to believe, but is it any more so than the experience of another Christian, the apostle Paul? Paul did not want to boast of his experiences, but the Corinthians forced him to do so. He then described his visions and revelations this way:

> I know a man in Christ who fourteen years ago—
> whether in the body I do not know, or out of the
> body I do not know, God knows—such a man
> was caught up to the third heaven. And I know
> how such a man—whether in the body or apart
> from the body I do not know, God knows—was
> caught up into Paradise, and heard inexpressible
> words, which a man is not permitted to speak.
>
> (2 Corinthians 12:2–4)

God may have spoken to Ivan in such an unusual way— and perhaps to other Christians over the centuries— because Ivan had suffered much and would be suffering even more. The angel may have shown him the new Jerusalem to let him know there was a place he was going that would make all the suffering worthwhile.

I once asked a friend from India, who had had many experiences with angels, why we Americans so seldom see them. "If you need money," he said, "you pull out a credit

*Vanya , Myrna Grant, Creation House, 1974, pp. 62–65.

card. If you need protection, you call the police. If you need a friend, you go to the telephone. Those who do not have access to such help, but trust in God, are those who receive supernatural help."

Perhaps it is true that we in the Western world are accustomed to leaning heavily on every other kind of help *except* the supernatural. If so, we need to be willing to go beyond our resources, as God calls us, and find the help He promises.

In the comfortable circumstances in which many of us are living, we may catch fleeting glimpses of angels. The Scripture says this about angels: "Are they not all ministering spirits, sent out to render service for the sake of those who will inherit salvation?" (Hebrews 1:14).

Down through history God has spoken to many through angels. There is no reason to believe such angelic activity has now ceased, and abundant evidence to the contrary. Just don't be surprised if it happens to you!

13

Hearing Him As a Couple

What a delight it is for a husband and wife in harmony with each other to pray together! It is a double blessing for them to listen together to what God has to say about family needs and desires, and share it with each other. There are many special advantages of listening to God together. When illness comes, for example, a husband and wife are already united in their trust in God. They can now wait on God for His special direction.

God has given Lillie and me forty-two rich years of marriage. The first great treasure we received was the joy of being able to read the Bible and pray together. Next we began to listen to God together, and learn to hear Him speak to us. Then I began keeping a journal of my spiritual experiences. I can now go back over twenty years of journal records to see how often God has spoken to us. We can check to see how accurately we were hearing Him; when we were doing wishful thinking; and when God was really speaking to us.

In this process I have learned something important about the complementary relationship between husband and wife, which has a direct bearing on hearing God. Partners are often attracted to one another because of differences in personality traits. One sees strength in the other to compensate for his or her own weakness in that area. He or she may be strong in reasoning and logic but weak in sympathy and human relationships. The other may make peace naturally but find it difficult to organize and plan. One may have great vision of the future but little patience to work out the details to arrive at that goal. The other may be able to accomplish the most intricate and detailed tasks but cannot see beyond the immediate situation.

All these positive traits are God-given and good. We attract one another through them. Yet it may take us years to be able to understand these traits in each other. When I spent some time with my parents around their sixtieth anniversary, I observed their great love for and dependence on each other. But I also heard Dad say about some little action of Mother's, "I don't know why your mother does it that way." Mother offered her own defensive explanation of Dad: "You know that's the way your father is." It was done in love but also in recognition of the fact that there were traits in each other that even after sixty years they did not understand.

What husbands and wives do not always realize is that their understanding of one another affects even their ability to hear God—whether individually or as a couple.

When we are first put into close relationship with our spouse, for instance, his or her strengths can become an irritation to us. That often causes anger and threatens to drive us apart, and when we quarrel or judge one another, we are not likely to hear much of what God is saying. We need to recognize that our mate's strength is a God-given trait natural to him or her, and stop our judgment and criticism.

When a strong trait in another upsets us exceedingly, it is usually because it points out the *weakness* of that trait in us. If we are willing to acknowledge that fact, then we can offer forgiveness to the other and not only accept him or her but also begin to integrate that trait into our own character. This is the beginning of the character-building process, and of being able to hear God as a couple.

The apostle Peter describes how the husband and wife are to relate to each other so that their prayers are not hindered (see 1 Peter 3:1–7). The apostle Paul describes the love relationship between husband and wife (Ephesians 5:22–33) in preparation for putting on the whole armor of God, in order to stand against the schemes of the devil and "against the rulers, against the powers, against the world-forces of this darkness, against the spiritual forces of wickedness in the heavenly places" (Ephesians 6:12).

So it all fits together. By accepting one another and allowing God to speak through the other's personality, we add another antenna to our spiritual hearing device. First, we want God to speak to us through Scripture. We pray, confess our sins, and ask God to cleanse our hearts and minds. Then, because Jesus said, "My sheep hear My voice, and I know them, and they follow Me" (John 10:27), we prepare our hearts through worship and listening.

As we learned earlier, the voice of God may come in a hundred different ways. So, as husband and wife, we lay aside all preconceived ideas, as well as the expectation that a message will come the same to each of us. We accept what comes to us by the still, small voice, by impression, by vision, by word, or by Scripture. Not that we take every word or impression as being from God, for it is yet to be tested, but we accept in the same way as a motion is accepted in a business meeting—so that it can be discussed.

Lillie and I seldom receive a word from the Lord in the same way. At first that was hard to accept. We wasted much time because Lillie would receive a flow of words, while it never came to me that way. She had to learn to accept this as the way God often spoke to her, while I had to realize that I too could be receiving something—albeit shorter—from the Lord. I received more insight and direction, on the other hand, through dreams. Or sometimes I would simply ask a series of questions and receive a response from the Lord in the answers, which often came by inner impression. Gradually Lillie and I learned to trust God to speak to us, each in our own way.

We did not receive something specific every time we prayed and waited upon God. Sometimes we simply had the impression that all was well and the Lord had been with us. But the times we did hear something, we were careful to write down what we received. By writing down any impressions or messages, we had something concrete to deal with. And if they later proved to be a word from the Lord, we had a record to which we could go for verification.

Keeping a written record of prayer-listening times together has many advantages. It is amazing how quickly we forget a word of encouragement God has given us. Time after time I go back to my spiritual journal to review the events of my life, dreams and their interpretation as I received them, messages from Scripture, or words God gave me privately or us together. By looking back at that record, I remember the lessons God has taught us so that we do not need to relearn them.

The procedure Lillie and I follow goes something like this: After we have allowed each other time for silence and listening, and when we see that we have each had a chance to write down what we have received, we then exchange the messages. Sometimes we are a bit anxious; one may wonder if the other has received a contradictory word. But as long as we are in harmony with each other and with God, this seldom happens.

One day it did seem to happen. A neighboring pastor told me he was planning to go to Haiti where three hundred national pastors would be gathering for a conference. He asked if I would go with him and share in the ministry. My heart leaped at the opportunity and I responded with a tentative yes, assuming Lillie and I would be given a go-ahead from the Lord.

When I got home and told Lillie about the invitation, she got the immediate impression I should not go on that trip. And the next day we prayed about it and waited on the Lord.

"Herman, I still do not think you should go on that trip," she said, to my surprise.

"But there are three hundred pastors gathering for that conference from many parts of Haiti. I believe we have a responsibility to meet that need."

We prayed and listened again and again, with the same results. Finally one day Lillie said, "Herman, I think you should go after all."

What a relief! What she did *not* tell me was that as soon as she endorsed my going, she felt uneasy about her decision. But she did not want to reverse herself immediately, so she waited until the next day.

Then, after our regular prayer time, she said, "We have always been in harmony, Herman, and I've felt so bad about disagreeing with you that I felt I must be wrong in my impression. But ever since I said that to you yesterday, I've had such uneasiness that I think I was wrong in endorsing the trip."

When I saw how seriously she had been wrestling with this question, I said, "If that's the case, Lillie, then I need to check my guidance."

As I became quiet before the Lord, I suddenly recognized something I had not been aware of before: It was not the Lord but my sympathy for those Haitian pastors telling me to go. God often uses sympathy for those in need, but sympathy is not necessarily the voice of the Lord; nor does the need, as Oswald Chambers points out, constitute the call.

So I canceled out of this trip. Later, when the pastor in charge of the conference returned, he confided to me: "Things did not turn out at all as we had planned, Herman. It's a good thing you didn't go with us."

It was another lesson to me in hearing the voice of God—the importance of being in harmony with your prayer partner. Now Lillie and I never act without being in agreement. After all, the same Holy Spirit dwells in both of us. He will not contradict Himself; He will say the same thing to both of us, just in different ways.

14

Hearing Him In a Group

My personal lessons in group listening began at a time of great crisis, when Lillie and I desperately needed the help and direction of the Lord.

I had received Christ into my life at the age of eleven, and in my college days knelt quietly beside my bed and yielded my life to the Holy Spirit. If I did that, I was told, I would experience new power for victory over sin, and be conscious of the personal direction of the Holy Spirit in my life. In a quiet but real way, these things began to happen in my life.

But during my twenty-five years as a Baptist pastor, I had sought the Lord earnestly to find power for my ministry. For the last two months I had even been meeting with a pastor friend for prayer. We prayed two full hours each day to find the power that would change lives, as I saw it described in the book of Acts. I did not know that old barriers from years of training were blocking the way of God's power.

Then our world was turned upside-down as our daughter disappeared in the middle of the night. We began to seek the Lord in greater earnestness. Even when we found our daughter, I could not offer her the help I should have been able to give. A flood of doubts swept through my old theological framework and made me question the structure that had been built around me.

I knew the foundation was in Jesus Christ, and that was solid. My home training had been good and that remained. Much of the teaching I had received in preparation for the ministry also stood the test. But there was one area in question: Was not the power of the Holy Spirit, as evidenced in the early Church, being expressed today in ways we had been taught to shun? I had to look again.

When I finally yielded myself to the Holy Spirit in any way He wanted to express Himself, I was filled with great joy, and power came to me and others in the church. But like the new wine that cannot be contained in old wineskins (Matthew 9:17), so my new joy and power could hardly be contained in the old encrusted doctrines of the church. Both my ministry and my teaching were challenged. In fact, the church called an important meeting to decide whether to relieve me of my pastoral call.

It was at this time that Lillie and I met a man who told us about his prayer group. The members of this group were well-disciplined, having met together once a week for about five years. Lillie and I, hungry for God's leading about the church situation, decided to attend a meeting just one night before the all-important church meeting.

When we arrived, we were unknown to all but the one friend. The group gathered in an informal manner, some sitting on the floor and some in chairs. I offered to explain why I had come, in order to make my request for prayer. But one of the men suggested it was better that I not do so. That surprised me. I had never been to a prayer meeting like this before.

After informal conversation, some members of the group began to read the Scriptures. Some were quiet in meditation and some offered audible prayer. Then one of the women had a vision of a belt that had many fancy ornaments attached. She said she did not know what the vision represented. Then a man, after prayer, gave us an interpretation. Lillie and I were to let go of the security we were holding onto. And before the evening was over, we were told just how we should conduct ourselves the next evening at the church meeting, which would prove to go against us.

God gave us great peace about the direction that came from that group, even though those present had had no idea we were facing such a crisis decision in our lives. Later one of them commented: "Isn't it much better that you didn't tell us your problem? You can see for yourself that it is God who has spoken to you through us."

They also pointed out how one of them had had a vision, another a Scripture, another a prophetic word from God. Another of the members had received neither a word nor a vision, yet had provided a solid confirmation of what had been given. Each person had a vital part to play and each was allowed to contribute what the Lord gave. What's more, I knew if there had not been unity within the group, they would not have proceeded with any action.

The advice the group gave to us that evening proved to be wise counsel indeed. We trusted the Lord's direction through them and obeyed it, for we had peace within our hearts that it was not only scriptural but that the Spirit of God had confirmed it.

The Lord gave us that same marvelous peace at the

church meeting the next night. By that time, I had yielded up my security in the outward organization and put my trust in God to take care of us.

What the prayer group members suggested did, in fact, come to pass. But by being prepared beforehand, we allowed God to take control of the meeting. When the final decision by the church went against us and we were dismissed, I could still pray for God to turn it into good for the church. For Lillie and me, it proved to be a release to an exciting new ministry.

Any group that gathers to hear God needs to have a deep sense of gathering around the Lord and not around any one person, or even around a need or problem. God must be given the freedom to change the agenda and turn everyone's attention to something that is more important, as He sees fit. The unity of the group does not come from the fact that the members all have a common need, but rather that they have a common Lord.

I do not believe this kind of group listening will work unless all members have the Holy Spirit indwelling them. Members of such a group, therefore, should be Christians by spiritual rebirth, not in name only; then the Holy Spirit can bind them together into a unity in Christ.

We are not to try to force a unity among believers, for God has already made His children one. Rather, "with all humility and gentleness, with patience, showing forbearance to one another in love, [we are to] *preserve* the unity of the Spirit in the bond of peace" (Ephesians 4:2–3, italics added). If there is discord among the members of a group (just as between husband and wife), it is difficult for God's Spirit to convey God's message to that group.

It is important that we learn to submit to one another in a group concerning the gifts He gave us. If ever the love described in 1 Corinthians 13 is important, it is when the Church receives the gifts or manifestations of the Holy Spirit. Note that Paul's description of this love is actually sandwiched between two chapters that describe the exercise of the gifts of the Spirit.

The pattern for developing group unity is found in the Scriptures. The members of the growing church in Jerusalem "were continually devoting themselves to the apostles' teaching and to fellowship, to the breaking of bread and to prayer" (Acts 2:42). And in the midst of this fellowship, God spoke to them and directed their witness for Him.

We have had much exhortation to pray more, but if we pray and do not listen, we hear only ourselves speaking. This not only gets monotonous; it brings death to a church. To listen and hear God speak, on the other hand, brings excitement, for His word may come to one or another of us, while the Spirit of God in *each* believer confirms what is from Him. Again, I recommend keeping pen and paper handy, and writing down what the Lord seems to be saying. This provides an opportunity to test the word that comes, and also to remember what is given.

As we learn to listen, we will recognize that many things crowd into our thinking that are neither necessarily of the Lord nor of the evil one. They are simply things of self with which we are preoccupied. Two principles here are important. First, the Lord will confirm any word He gives us. And second, the one for whom the vision is given is the one who has the right of interpretation. A vision or word of the Lord that comes to us through someone else—as the vision of the maple tree came in Canada for Lillie and me—should only confirm what we already know in our hearts, though we may not have been aware of it. When we receive it in this way, we will recognize if it is for us.

It is very important that we do not accept someone else's interpretation if our hearts do not respond to it (though this is not to say we will *like* it). It is also important not to force a message of prophecy or direction, or an interpretation of a vision or dream, upon another whose heart does not answer to it. Let the Spirit of God confirm His own word to another's heart without our pressure.

There is often more safety in group listening than in our own private hearing, so long as there is humble submission to one another and a community of love within the group. It is possible for a group to become just as rigid as an individual, especially if that group has been meeting for a long time receiving helpful guidance. There is a danger for them to think they have found the *only* way to receive a word from God—which is why it is as important for a group to submit to a larger group for correction, as it is for an individual to submit to a group.

I have found group listening to be a safe way to learn to hear the voice of God. This protects us from our own bias or strong desires that would steer us off-course. God is more than willing to teach us how to hear His voice if we cooperate in faith, believing that He can speak to us, and in humility are willing to submit our guidance for testing.

All guidance must be tested, as we shall see, since we are all learning to communicate in the spiritual realm. Only then can we expect to find communication with God that is reliable.

15 Testing What I Hear

It is exciting to know we can hear the voice of God speaking to us! That is a special privilege given to the children of God. But once we have been persuaded that we, like the men and women of the Bible, can hear God speak, we must learn to test the voices we hear so that we can discern which is really the voice of God.

There are many reasons why we must do this. First, we may become so excited when we begin to recognize God's voice that we run into the danger of believing that everything we hear is from God. This is the error some Christians make when they say the Lord told them things that do not prove to be from the Lord at all.

A second danger is that when we have heard the voice of God a few times and it has proven true, pride may enter in and we may believe we can hear the voice of God perfectly. We may have heard it accurately at certain times, but to say we can hear God perfectly is to say that we have no prejudice, no bias, no imbalance—in other words, no sin.

There is only One who could say that: Jesus, the Son of God. Until we come to His perfection, we will always need to test our hearing and our seeing.

A third reason for testing what we hear is that too much

is involved to leave accuracy to chance. While it is true that
God's voice guides obedient listeners today as it did in
Bible times, we also find plenty of mental patients who
think they are "messengers." So for the sake of our
testimony to the world, as well as for our own spiritual
safety, we must test what we claim to hear from God.

Fourth, any message needs to be tested for the sake of
preserving what God has given us. Samuel said, "Let none
of [the words of God] fall to the ground" (1 Samuel 3:19).
There was a dearth of people in those days who heard from
God. Our world today, amid hopelessness, war, crime, and
suffering, longs for words that transcend the natural. A
church without a fresh word from God runs along the dry
channel of tradition. And consider how desperately we
ourselves seek a word from God when our troubles have
brought us to the very end of ourselves—that is, to the end
of our wisdom, our courage, our hope. A word from God at
such times is worth more than money can buy.

Fifth, we need to test what we hear because of the very
nature of our hearing. We may have the idea that we hear
God just as clearly as we hear another person, but we do
not even hear each other well; how much less are we apt to
hear God correctly! Besides, we hear God not with our
physical ears but with our spirits. What determines
whether the voice is God's is not its loudness, but rather
our spirits that must be tuned to His Spirit.

The truth is, we know very little about the human spirit,
and we have much to learn about its hearing ability. In
fact, we might marvel that we are able to hear God at all.
It is a little like our ability to hear the radio or watch
television without knowing much about how either instru-

ment works. God is immortal, eternal, invisible. He is
Spirit while we are physical. It is incredible that without
much understanding we can begin to hear God! This very
fact demands that we test what we hear.

Although we "hear" with our spirits, our physical bodies
also become involved in the process. When we are tired, we
are not as likely to respond to a word that demands action
of us, and when we are not feeling up to par physically, we
are perhaps too absorbed with our discomfort to hear very
well. Others may hear the Lord better than the tired or sick
person.

Even more subtle than the effects of our physical body
on our spiritual hearing is the fact that our whole
personality enters into the hearing process. Our mind, will,
and emotions all affect our spiritual hearing. A rational
thinker tends to believe that if a word sounds reasonable, it
is most likely from the Lord. Unfortunately, some churches
have been run in just that way—the way a successful
businessman might run his business. But God is not
limited to man's reason. He uses it when He can direct it.

Other people are highly influenced by their emotions. At
one time they get excited about doing great things, and at
other times they grow discouraged over the slightest
problem. Some may be influenced by their feelings to the
extent that they are bound by the feelings of others. It is
good to be sensitive, but when it keeps us from expressing
ourselves, it may also keep us from hearing the Lord
properly.

Some people observe the natural realm so intently that
they have difficulty seeing the spiritual realm. To them,
only things they can observe with their five senses are facts.

The figures they see in their account books obstruct their ability to see anything that goes beyond, and the fear of the supernatural may prevent them from hearing God's promises.

The strongly intuitive person may think he is the one who really hears God. Elijah was probably like that. He often heard what others could not hear. But when he suggested he was the only one who heard God speak, God reminded him of seven thousand others who also had not bowed their knees to Baal.

Along with all the potential of the intuitive person, there are also real dangers. They, along with the rest of us, need to persist in the process of maturation. Few of us are fully balanced, and as long as our personalities are not fully developed, our ability to hear God will also be imperfect. This is true no matter how strongly developed our sensory faculties, or powers of reason, or feelings or intuition. Humility before God and others is the safest protection against the subtle temptations of pride.

A sixth reason for testing what we hear is that so few of us know the Scriptures well. Many are swayed easily by wrong interpretations of Scripture. But since the same Holy Spirit who inspired the Scriptures is the One who correctly interprets them to us, we need to be careful to check anything we hear with God's principles that are borne out in the Bible.

The apostle John tells us of the danger of false teachers, and that to test their message we need to find out whether the Holy Spirit gave it. "Every spirit that confesses that Jesus Christ has come in the flesh is from God," John declared, "and every spirit that does not confess Jesus is not from God; and this is the spirit of the antichrist" (1 John 4:2-3).

Finally, we must test the voices that we hear because Satan will try to imitate the voice of God. He is a master at imitation. But there are three ways to recognize the Deceiver. First, we can check to see if what he says agrees with Scripture. Second, as John tells us, we can recognize him by his attitude toward Jesus Christ, for Satan will not admit that Jesus has really come from God and become man. And third, we can recognize him through the gift of discernment given us by the Spirit of God. The spirit within a Christian often recognizes an evil spirit, even though that evil spirit may speak deceptively beautiful words.

So among the many voices that we hear, such as the voice of our own desires, the voice of public opinion, the voice of authority, and the voice of temptation, comes the voice of God. We must test every voice we hear to determine whether it comes from us, or from our enemy, or from God.

Loren Cunningham, the founder of Youth With A Mission, recounts the many times he has raised the question "Is that really You, God?"* Once, before arriving in New Zealand with much work before him, he asked, "God, do You want me to go on a fast?"

Immediately an answer rushed into his brain: *Yes, and I want you to withdraw from people for seven days, starting when you arrive.*

Is That Really You, God? Loren Cunningham. Chosen Books.

Cunningham was dumfounded. There was so much to do! "Am I hearing You right, God?" he asked. "Is that really You?" The only answer he got was a quiet reaffirmation.

But obedience to that voice proved to be a turning point for the work of the mission.

When Loren Cunningham returned to California, he came down with the flu. While nursing his aches and fever, a thought came into his mind: *You are to have a school. It is to be called a School of Evangelism.*

Loren wondered if this was from God. Then another thought cut through: *Your school is to be in Switzerland.*

Switzerland! "Is this You, God?"

When Loren told his wife about this, they decided to scout things out in Switzerland the following spring, using their "nest egg" house in California as collateral for a loan to get tickets. But Loren still wondered if the Switzerland idea was really from God. He wanted reassurance that he had, in fact, been hearing His voice.

Two days before the Cunninghams were to leave, Loren got an unexpected invitation to breakfast from his friend Willard Cantelon.

"Loren, I have a message for you," Willard said. "The Lord has been planting the idea in my mind that someone should start a school in Switzerland. Last night He told me you are to be the one."

Just the confirmation from a trusted friend that Loren needed!

The key to Loren Cunningham's successful program, which now reaches many countries with thousands of youths and volunteers, is that whenever Loren thought he

heard from the Lord, he asked, "Is that really You, God?"
Then he waited for confirmation of the Lord's voice.

We may well ask, "How can we test the many voices we
hear to discern which is the voice of God?" Scripture
suggests three tests: an individual test; a test by the local
and the larger church; and a test by the Church universal—that is, the Bible. Each of these tests checks our
relationship with Jesus Christ, our relationship to the local
church, and our relationship to the Church at large.

The individual test is suggested by Paul in his letter to
the Colossians: "Let the peace of Christ rule in your hearts,
to which indeed you were called in one body" (Colossians
3:15). To let the peace of Christ rule is to let it govern or be
the referee.

The peace of God is a gift that Jesus promised: "Peace I
leave with you; My peace I give to you; not as the world
gives, do I give to you" (John 14:27). And He goes on to
tell us not to be troubled or afraid. As Jesus said, this kind
of peace is not available from the world. It is a precious gift
to the followers of the Lord Jesus Christ, which comes
straight from the Holy Spirit.

When we are in fellowship with God, this peace guards
our hearts and minds, as Paul says: "The peace of God,
which surpasses all comprehension, shall guard your
hearts and your minds in Christ Jesus" (Philippians 4:7).
The word *guard* is a military word that speaks of protection
by guards at the gates. God's peace will protect both our
hearts (our deep unconscious) and our minds (our conscious selves). Paul says we are to let that peace rule—be
referee or umpire—in our hearts.

God knows it is not always easy for us to know whether

the words we hear are from Him or from ourselves. So He gives us the assurance that as long as we walk in His way, we will be kept in peace, but that if we step out of His way, His peace will leave us. Disobedience or unbelief will deprive us of peace. And if we follow a voice that is not God's voice, His peace will begin to dissolve—a signal that something is wrong.

Then there is the test by the local church. We dare not go long without checking our guidance with other Christians. The apostle Paul has given us a basic principle to follow: "Of the prophets, two or three may speak, while the rest exercise their judgment upon what is said" (1 Corinthians 14:29, NEB). To "exercise judgment" here means to investigate, to interrogate, or to determine.

Paul also wrote: "Do not quench the Spirit; do not despise prophetic utterances. But examine everything carefully; hold fast to that which is good" (1 Thessalonians 5:19–21). The local church must learn, therefore, to test the word that comes to it through its members.

But a church is often divided and always fallible. How can we test our guidance through it? To function properly as a discerning body, a church must be in submission to the Lord and His work. It must also be in harmony within itself, for the Spirit of God cannot easily be heard in the midst of confusion and rivalry.

In any body there will be differences of personality, but together the members can probably come to a balanced decision. The members of a local church will probably also discern evil forces with which the individual may not be acquainted. This, too provides protection.

When we find part of the body of Christ that is in

obedience to the Lord with the members in fellowship with one another, we can take our guidance to that group for testing. The same Holy Spirit who indwells us also indwells other members of that body. Those members can listen to the Spirit and see if He is saying the same thing to them as He is to us. This is the way the test of discernment works through the local body of Christ.

The author of the book of Hebrews offers this overall picture:

> Everyone who partakes only of milk is not accustomed to the word of righteousness, for he is a babe. But solid food is for the mature, who because of practice have their senses trained to discern good and evil.
>
> (Hebrews 5:13–14)

Along with the test of the local church is the test of the larger church. We may receive this by going beyond our local church or denomination, since denominational doctrines (while generally stating great truths) also tend to hem in its members. It is of great value for us to listen to Christians of different denominational backgrounds who also submit themselves to Jesus Christ. The Spirit of God living in us witnesses to the Spirit within them, and to the truths we may interpret differently.

We have been divided along denominational lines for many years. Do we dare to think that God has taught only us, and not others, the great truths of the Christian faith? He teaches all who submit themselves to His Lordship, though most of us comply only in part. How refreshing it is to spend time in discussion and quiet meditation and prayer with those of another doctrinal persuasion, and to listen to God through them! We benefit as we see truths from a different perspective.

We desperately need this kind of correction. God has hidden nuggets of truth in all believers, which we will find when we listen and share. Without this kind of balance, we may interpret a word from the Lord with too much of the bias of our own tradition. Praise God that He, by His Spirit, is bringing us together, so that we can listen to God through one another!

God is a God of order and not of confusion. But He is not subject to *our* order, either of class, race, doctrine, or philosophy. He has a higher order, crossing all the boundaries we devise. Just as God has made one world, and we have divided it into many nations, defending and fighting over their boundaries, so God has ordered universal Truth. Yet it has been divided up by many denominations, each defending its own doctrinal borders. In the midst of this we are to submit to God's order, so that if He speaks a word to us, that word may be tested not by our prejudice but by the Holy Spirit in His whole Body.

Beyond the individual test, and the tests through the local and the larger church, there is the proving ground of the Church universal. The experiences of believers over thousands of years have been brought together in the form we now know as the Scriptures. Since the Church through the ages has recognized these records and messages to be applicable to all, it is vital for us to measure ourselves by them.

Through the Scriptures we can check our guidance with believers from many cultures and languages who heard from God over a period of sixteen centuries. Their experiences become a pattern for us when they heard God rightly, and a warning for us when they failed. Thus, the study of the Scriptures is basic to our understanding of God's guidance to us.

In fact, we must not only study it but meditate upon it— to learn how, for instance, Elijah could stand before the wicked king Ahab and declare that it would not rain until he said the word. Or how Daniel, a captive slave, could declare to Nebuchadnezzar, that great monarch of Babylon, the interpretation of a dream that the king had forgotten, and earn such respect from the king as to be elevated to president of that kingdom. The Scriptures give us a reliable pattern to follow to hear the word of the Lord.

Our great and final test is to see if what we hear is in agreement with the principles of Scripture. If we were to receive a personal word of guidance that violated any one of the Ten Commandments, given by God through Moses, we would know we had not "heard" correctly. God will never say one thing in His written commandments and something else in private.

Jesus interpreted the commandments even more fully than religious leaders did in Old Testament times, but never in contradiction. We must check our understanding, therefore, with what Jesus said. Besides, we have the teaching of the apostles and prophets to help direct our way. We may also compare our experiences with the experiences of people described in the Bible. Throughout the Scriptures we find principles for our guidance.

Satan will try to deceive us by quoting Scripture out of context, so we need to know more of the Scriptures than enough merely to prove a point. There are principles to be found in the Word of God that we must heed as we walk in the way of the Lord. To live by the Word of God, we must meditate on it in the way that God told Joshua: "This book of the law shall not depart from your mouth, but you shall meditate on it day and night, so that you may be careful to do according to all that is written in it; for then you shall make your way prosperous, and then you will have success" (Joshua 1:8). Through meditation on the Scriptures, we come to understand the deeper truths hidden in the Word of God. In this way we come to hear God more clearly, for in the Scriptures is hidden the wisdom of God.

If industry spends years of effort and millions of dollars in research in order to learn the secret laws hidden in the universe, how much more do we need to learn the spiritual laws God has put into His Word. Jesus said, "The Father loves the Son, and shows Him all things that He Himself is doing" (John 5:20). If Jesus learned to listen to the Father and be obedient, we too must learn to listen carefully and without fear, for God still speaks to His people.

Finally, then, we must test every message that seems to come from the Lord, whether by voice, vision, dream, prophecy, revelation, or something else. In our everyday experience, we test it by the peace God gives us as we walk honestly in His way. On more important occasions we may invite a portion of the local church to discern whether it is a true message from God, or whether much of it—even all of it—comes from ourselves. And at all times we test it with the Church universal by going to the Scriptures.

In these ways we will be kept from the deceit of the enemy and from the selfish desires that divert us from hearing God's voice.

16

Obedience to What I Hear

Author Nita Scoggan in her book *Pillars of the Pentagon* recounts the story of a friend who was having severe financial problems. This friend drove to work one day with the gas gauge practically on empty. That night she asked God to help her get home and provide for her children. But traffic was heavy. Sitting in bumper-to-bumper traffic burned up a lot of gas, while fearful thoughts flooded into her mind. She didn't even have money for a phone call if her car quit. Could she get clear across town to her home?

No gas. No money. Hardly any food for dinner.

"Thank You, Lord, that Your Word says You will supply all my needs through Christ Jesus," she murmured, and pushed the doubts from her mind.

Then she heard God speaking to her, right there in traffic: *Go home and take all the food you have in your house to Mrs. W. right away.*

"But Lord," she protested, "I don't have enough food for our dinner and Mrs. W. lives back across town! The car is running on fumes already."

Gather all you have and take it to Mrs. W. You will be blessed.

When she got home, her children were puzzled to see their mom going through cupboards and filling a bag with odds and ends of food items. Instead of fixing dinner, she told her children she had to go and see Mrs. W., a widow who was sick and lived on the other side of town.

"Do your homework and pray for me, children," she said. "God told me to go and I'm going. He's going to bless us. I know it." And off she went.

It was almost dark when her car pulled up at the widow's address. As she got out of the car, she heard God's voice say, *Look down at your feet.*

She did look down. At her feet was a muddy mass of fallen leaves.

The words came again. *Look at your feet.*

Still all she saw were muddy leaves. She bent down and picked up the little clump near her feet. It was not leaves, but money covered with mud! She stuck it in her pocket, grabbed the groceries, and went in to see Mrs. W. They prayed together, and promising she would be back soon to visit, the woman left for home and her children.

Her first stop was the nearest gas station. She didn't even know how much money she had found. She took the clump from her pocket and saw a ten-dollar bill on top. That almost filled up the tank. "Thank You, Jesus!"

Next stop, the grocery store. Inside she counted the money—$300! She bought just enough items for dinner, breakfast, and lunch, since she couldn't wait to get home.

"Come in the kitchen, children," she announced on her arrival, "and see what the Lord has done! I had to go clear across town to get my blessing from God."*

Pillars of the Pentagon, Nita Scoggan. Royalty Publishing House, pp. 139–40.

Her blessing would not have come if she had not obeyed God's voice. Nita Scoggan's friend had discovered a vital truth: that the key to knowing God's will is obedience. Jesus said, "If any man is willing to do [God's] will, he shall know of [My] teaching, whether it is of God" (John 7:17). If we do not obey what we know to be true, we will soon be confused about the will of God. We will vacillate. Things will appear out-of-focus.

Nothing will bring guidance into focus, on the other hand, better than obedience.

At times we may find nothing wrong when we test our guidance, but neither are we fully persuaded that what we have received is God's specific direction. In those instances, before acting on whatever it is, we need to seek confirmation. This may come through Scripture, through a word that a friend says to us, through a sermon, or through events that convince us that what we have heard is really from the Lord.

Dean, a professor of oceanography, told me: "When I get an impression to do something, I find that one of the indications it's from the Lord is that it is fortified by other circumstances. I was meeting once with a student at lunch hour. While we were talking I felt led to pray for him. When I obeyed this impression, I found I had privacy, that there were no interruptions, and that the circumstances were right."

There is one more thing we can do when we have listened as carefully as we can but still are not sure the voice or impression or direction is really from God: We can ask God for a sign of His confirmation. As I see the pattern in Scripture, God does not mind our asking for a sign to reassure us, since He really wants us to know His will and the right thing to do. He is willing to make the way clear and prove Himself, if we are willing to stay with Him.

In asking for a sign of God's confirmation, however, our hearts must be right. We must be seeking His will, and glory in His name, not in the sign itself. Further, I find it safe to ask God whether He wants to give a sign confirming His guidance. That protects us from asking for some foolish thing that God cannot give without violating His basic laws. So long as pride does not enter into our motives, God is usually quite willing to respond to our request for encouragement.

Look in another way at the familiar story of Gideon. When Israel lay conquered and in slavery to the Midianites, the angel of the Lord appeared to Gideon as he worked in the field, and told him he had been appointed by God to deliver Israel. Gideon was a young farmer—not a general or even a soldier. He was startled by the angel's words and not sure it was really God speaking to him. So he said to God:

> If now I have found favor in Thy sight, then show me a sign that it is Thou who speakest with me. Please do not depart from here, until I come back to Thee.
>
> (Judges 6:17)

Then Gideon went home and prepared a young goat for an offering, which the angel told him to place on a rock. When Gideon did so, the angel touched the meat and bread with his staff, and fire flamed up from the rock and consumed them. Then, just as suddenly, the angel was gone.

This confirmation by a miracle satisfied Gideon for only a short time. Then he said to God:

> I will put a fleece of wool on the threshing floor. If there is dew on the fleece only, and it is dry on all the ground, then I will know that Thou wilt deliver Israel through me, as Thou hast spoken.
>
> (Judges 6:37)

That night it happened exactly as he had asked. But, as we all know, Gideon was still not sure of himself, so he asked for the same sign in reverse, adding, "Please don't be angry with me."

What is not often noted is that God was *not* angry with Gideon for asking for these repeated signs. In fact, He even encouraged him to ask for another sign when he went to battle. God was willing to give him all the signs he needed to assure him that it was really He, God, who was speaking.

He deals with us in the same way. He does not want to leave us in doubt and confusion when He gives us an assignment to do. But He does want our obedience.

The Lord demonstrated the same principle with Isaiah and King Ahaz. The king did not believe God would protect him from the two kings coming against him, so God sent him a message through Isaiah the prophet: "Ask a sign for yourself from the Lord your God; make it deep as Sheol or high as heaven" (Isaiah 7:11).

But Ahaz replied, "I will not ask, nor will I test the Lord!" (verse 12).

Isaiah was angry with the king that he would not ask for a sign from God, and said, "Is it too slight a thing for you to try the patience of men, that you will try the patience of my God as well?'' (verse 13). And God proceeded to offer His own sign to Ahaz.

Isaiah must have felt something like we would feel if someone refused to believe we would be faithful to perform our promise, and would not accept any sign of assurance.

We may wonder why Jesus did not give the Pharisees a sign when they asked for it (see Mark 8:11–12), but the reason is evident. They had all the signs they needed in the works and miracles He had already performed, and still they would not believe Him. Jesus knew it would do no good to give them more signs.

The distinction suggested here is important. When we need a sign for reassurance, God is quite willing to give it, but if we do not obey the evidence God gives us, He may refuse to give us more. If we honestly seek to do the will of God, then He is quite willing to confirm His word, even with a sign if necessary. But He is not about to play games with us.

There is a wonderful promise in Isaiah 30:19–21, which I believe we can apply to ourselves:

> He will surely be gracious to you at the sound of your cry; when He hears it, He will answer you. . . . He, your Teacher will no longer hide Himself, but your eyes will behold your Teacher. And your ears will hear a word behind you, "This is the way, walk in it," whenever you turn to the right or to the left.

We may not always understand God's guidance clearly, but if we venture out in faith and turn aside by mistake, we will hear His voice behind us saying, "No, not that way. This is the way; walk here."

The key to understanding what God is saying to us, then, is obedience. Only as we obey do we experience what God has for us. Abraham became a father of the faithful because he learned instant obedience to God's command. He did not learn it all at once. He hesitated at first, then went part of the way to the land to which he was called. He felt discouraged when the answers to God's promises were not fulfilled soon enough. He stumbled and fell many times, but gradually learned that God's way is the best way.

Along with his obedience, Abraham's faith grew, too. He found that God could be trusted, so bit by bit he trusted Him more.

It is good that the Bible gives us the whole story of Abraham's life. If we saw only his success at the end, we would become discouraged. If we saw him only offering up his son as a sacrifice to God, we might be put off and say, "I could never do that." But since God has given us a record of Abraham's gradual learning process, we are encouraged to try our own hand at Abraham's kind of obedient commitment.

We may say that if we could be sure what we heard was really God speaking, we would be less reluctant to obey. But one hundred percent assurance will never come. We can only do the best we can. We try to eliminate the voices that contradict the teaching and principles found in the Word of God. We take time for silent meditation to get in tune with God. We try to discern not only the sound or feeling or vision of what seems to be the voice of God, but also the harmony of our own spirit with the Spirit of God.

I have come to realize that in big decisions I want to be sure of the Lord's guidance, while in little things I will venture in directions I *think* are God's will, but prove not to be. I don't check them carefully enough. At least in these instances I learn what is not the voice of God or the will of God for me. Without venturing I would learn nothing.

When we keep in close fellowship with the Lord, He keeps us from the big mistakes while we learn in the little things. God's grace is wonderful to the one who trusts Him: "For a righteous man falls seven times, and rises again" (Proverbs 24:16). But I also pray with the psalmist, "Keep back Thy servant from presumptuous sins" (Psalm 19:13). These usually come from pride.

We will not always understand God's will clearly. " 'My thoughts are not your thoughts, neither are your ways My ways,' declares the Lord. 'For as the heavens are higher than the earth, so are My ways higher than your ways, and My thoughts than your thoughts' " (Isaiah 55:8–9). We often get only a veiled glimpse of what God has in mind, but He is patient and willing to teach us if we walk humbly and honestly before Him.

Obedience is the expression of faith and the key to learning to recognize God's voice ever more clearly. We need to be willing to risk those little mistakes as we venture in faith, and trust God to protect us from the big ones.

17

Keeping a Journal

In life we keep the treasures we value. Unwanted mail that comes is tossed away with just a glance. But bills, whether we like them or not, are carefully laid aside until we pay them. Checks are deposited in the bank so that no money is lost. Diplomas and certificates of recognition are hung on the wall for others to see.

What do we do with the promises the Lord gives us? They are worth more than any amount of money. What happens to the lessons we have learned through difficult and costly experiences? Too often we forget within a day or two the words of encouragement God gave us. The promises vanish away in the midst of new problems, unless we make a proper record of them.

I know by personal experience. Lillie and I pray for our children regularly, often for specific needs. Then we wait on the Lord for His answer, and graciously He gives us a word of encouragement.

Recently one of these words came to us: *Salvation shall spring forth like the grass and you will rejoice with joy unspeakable, for I will do what I have promised. Therefore, wait in patience and trust in Me, for I am faithful.*

This was an encouraging word and we did rejoice in it.

Just a few days later, however, I asked Lillie if she remembered what the promise was that God had given. She did not remember, and neither did I, for problems had absorbed our attention again. Since I keep a journal, however, we were able to check it, find the promise, and again receive encouragement.

Twenty years ago my journal was a meager record kept in a daily planning book. After three years I began to type out the handwritten notes. This year I have put them on a computer from which they are printed out.

The reason we have the Bible today is that men and women kept a record of their experiences with God. If David had not kept a record of the songs he wrote, we would not have the beautiful shepherd Psalm, greatly loved through the ages, as well as many other songs of joy and praise.

David kept a record of his trials, too. If he had not, we would never imagine the great King David barefoot before his armed men, fleeing his throne in Jerusalem from his own son, Absalom, who had raised a great conspiracy against him. All the city was in an uproar; the people covered their heads and wept. One old man came to bless him. Another came and cursed him, while yet another threw stones at him. Then word came that King David must cross the river Jordan before morning with the remnants of his army. In the midst of all that confusion David wrote:

> O Lord, how my adversaries have increased!
> Many are rising up against me.
> Many are saying of my soul,
> "There is no deliverance for him in God."

> But Thou, O Lord, art a shield about me,
> My glory, and the One who lifts my head.
> I was crying to the Lord with my voice,
> And He answered me from His holy mountain.
> [Selah.]

Then comes this remarkable statement in the midst of the fear and sorrow that surrounded him:

> I lay down and slept;
> I awoke, for the Lord sustains me,
> I will not be afraid of ten thousands of people
> Who have set themselves against me round about.
>
> (Psalm 3)

At another time King David fell into a different kind of danger. He took another man's wife, then sent her husband off on a mission that would kill him. He tried to cover up this sin, but failed. He wrote:

> When I kept silent about my sin, my body wasted
>   away
> Through my groaning all day long.
> For day and night Thy hand was heavy upon me;
> My vitality was drained away as with the fever-
>   heat of summer.
>
> (Psalm 32)

When David was finally confronted with his sin by the prophet Nathan, he made the great confession of Psalm 51. Although all these experiences of David were private and personal, he kept a record of them. And because he did, they have become a blessing to millions.

The prophets, likewise, kept a record of the prophecies God gave them concerning the nations. Because of that, we have the books of the prophets in the Bible. Daniel's journal records the dreams of the long conversations God had with King Nebuchadnezzar. The prophets recorded what they received and then studied the prophecies to see what they meant (see 1 Peter 1:10–12).

Some of the disciples wrote biographies of Jesus for their time, not knowing God would make them part of the Scriptures. Paul's letters were written to personal friends and church groups, but God planned them for us also. John was told to record his visions of future things and they have been studied ever since.

We often fail to put value on the little things God gives us, for we are unable to discern what God chooses to use for His glory. But we can at least record them in a journal. We need not publicize what we receive, but we do need to record it so we can turn back to it for encouragement. And we may never know how God wants to use what He gives us in private.

I urge you to begin keeping a journal, if you are not already doing so. What to include in a spiritual journal? One of the first things we may record in the day are our dreams, because they come before our work begins. We cannot determine the importance of a dream until we have seen the whole of it and listened to its message. We need to have pencil and paper handy, therefore, so that immediately upon awakening, before our minds begin to plan the activities of the day, we can catch the fleeting dream. As we work on the dream, we can record its interpretation and message for us.

Then we may record the Scripture through which God speaks to us that day. Since the journal is a record of our spiritual journeys, not simply a diary to record daily

activities, the events of the day will provide the setting for
the Lord's working. Therefore we listen to what God is
saying to our hearts. To do that we meditate on the
Scriptures, or we may sit in contemplation of our Lord
Himself. We need to learn to "waste time with the Lord,"
from the world's viewpoint, in order to hear what God
wants to say to us. We may then record any dialogue, or
the result of the direction we have received.

God is interested in all we are doing. We must never
segregate life into the spiritual and the secular. God wants
to be involved in all of it. He wants to make the secular life
spiritual and the spiritual life earthy, as Jesus did in the
Incarnation.

What makes my friend Frank's journal so appealing is
its earthiness. He thinks of himself as a slow learner in
spiritual things. But he has the courage to write what he
thinks and record what he knows is not from himself, what
seems to be coming from the Lord. Here are some of his
entries:

Dear Lord,
What a week. Thank You for being with us
through it all—Eric's tail-ending of the 280Z [a
car accident], the final putting to sleep of our cat,
Max, my program being in bad shape and the
customer coming in next week with a hammer,
and dear Kirk doing himself in at school. I thank
You for the right frame of mind to get through it,
and I thank You it wasn't one hundred times
worse, like it can be. Lord, I need Your wisdom
at work concerning the BCA project. You said, I

believe, You would bless the project. Have I missed it? Thank You for everything.

Love, Frank.

Dear Frank,
I watched, with interest, how your family handled its events this week. You all did well and all responses were normal. I'm sorry, too, about Max; he was a good cat. Do not think that his death meant your and Charlotte's prayers weren't heard and understood. The course of nature needed to be fulfilled and you needed the experience of wanting something very much, not getting it, and still holding your trust in Me.

Enjoy the long weekend with Charlotte. Cultivate her love. Fellowship together in Me and worship the Father in your hearts. Things at work will be okay, both for you and the customer. Continue to strive to look at the big picture so that things of the flesh will assume their proper proportion. I love you, Frank.

Jesus.

One of the values of a journal is remembering the Lord's dealings with us. It is said that if we do not learn from history, then history will repeat itself in our lives, with all its mistakes. Paul told the Corinthians they were to learn from the mistakes of Israel. We can learn from ours, too, if we know what they are.

Another value of a journal is checking the guidance we have received. We may be able to look back on a time we felt God led us, and see that things did not turn out as they should have if He had really been in charge. Thus we can evaluate our guidance and keep a watch on our motives, just as a mountain guide routinely checks his compass.

Great journals have been written that have challenged Christians for centuries. St. Augustine's journal has remained a classic for people of all denominations and helped many in their struggles.

Dick, an engineer, told me how that particular journal helped him: "I had been working on a personal problem for a long time without success. Then I was given St. Augustine's writings and read, 'You have a will, but it is divided. Part of it wants to go one way, and another part wants to go another.' Suddenly, as though a light went on in me, I knew what was wrong and my problem was resolved."

We need not strive for the perfect, but we can record God's dealings with us daily for our own encouragement. It is important that we do not let any of God's words of instruction, encouragement, or challenge be lost. If we count the value of God's messages to us, we will be encouraged to discipline ourselves to record them.

A journal will provide us the opportunity to dialogue with God, with others, and even with ourselves. The lessons God teaches us in the midst of our trials will be a blessing to others later as we share them. The journal itself will become a record of our transactions with God and the revelations He gives us of Himself in our hours of contemplation. The record will enable us to check our guidance over our years of listening to Him.

And in that way we can get a reliable record of God's voice to us, on which we and others can depend.